In Praise of the Tridentine Mass
and of
Latin, Language of the Church

IN PRAISE
of the
Tridentine Mass
and of
Latin,
Language of the Church

FR. ROBERTO SPATARO

Translated by Zachary Thomas
Foreword by Raymond Leo Cardinal Burke
Introduction by Patrick M. Owens

Angelico Press

Originally published in Italian as
Elogio della Messa Tridentina:
e del latino lingua della Chiesa
© Fede e Cultura
www.fedecultura.com

First published in the USA
by Angelico Press 2019
Copyright © Fr. Roberto Spataro 2019

For information, address:
Angelico Press, Ltd.
169 Monitor St.
Brooklyn, NY 11222
www.angelicopress.com

978-1-62138-461-8 pb
978-1-62138-462-5 hb
978-1-62138-463-2 ebook

Book and cover design
by Michael Schrauzer
Cover photograph by Tracy Dunne

CONTENTS

FOREWORD
Raymond Leo Cardinal Burke

DURING THE PERIOD OF THE implementation of the reforms desired by the Second Vatican Ecumenical Council, two great treasures of ecclesial life were seriously neglected and even at risk of being lost. These two treasures are intimately connected with each other. The first is the classical form of the Roman rite, in use since the time of Pope St Gregory the Great,[1] and the second is the Latin language by means of which this Rite is expressed and through which the Church has transmitted down through the centuries, in an unbroken line, her doctrine and her discipline.

The postconciliar reform altered the former to such a degree, especially by its reduction, that for many it was difficult to see the continuity between the *Vetus Ordo* and the *Novus Ordo* of Holy Mass. In fact, in a revolutionary way, some even believe that there is no relationship between the two forms of the Rite, and that the *Novus Ordo* is the restoration of the true ancient form of the Rite of Mass that had been lost over time with the *Vetus Ordo*. The situation has greatly deteriorated due to a long period of liturgical experimentation (any period of experimentation is too long!) that has brought with it serious deformations of the indisputable beauty of the Roman rite, as it has been known in the Church for so many centuries and which has steadfastly inspired the faithful to holiness of life, at times even heroic holiness.

---

1   Motu proprio *Summorum Pontificum, AAS* 99:777–79.

The second treasure was simply forgotten as something no longer important. Because of the general indifference towards the teaching of Latin, especially in the seminaries, the Church has reached a state in which many of her pastors no longer know her universal language. If it is absurd to think that seminarians may seriously study theology, the sacred liturgy, and canon law without being able to read the primary texts written in Latin, it is even more absurd that priests destined for higher studies of the sacred sciences find themselves without this capacity. As a canonist, it makes no sense to me that someone charged with cultivating ecclesiastical discipline would be unable to read the norms of the law in their original form, not to mention the necessary direct knowledge of the sources of the law. It is particularly sad to confirm the fact that priests, whose primary work is the celebration of Holy Mass, are not able, because of the gaps in their formation, to access the beautiful texts of the *Missale Romanum*. I know first-hand of the pain of priests who would like to offer Holy Mass in Latin, both in the ordinary form and in the extraordinary form of the Roman rite, but do not have sufficient knowledge of Latin to do so.

Indifference and even contempt for the traditional form of the Roman rite naturally brought with it very serious effects in every aspect of ecclesial life, because the sacred liturgy, as the Fathers of the Second Vatican Council teach, is the source and summit (*fons et culmen*) of the whole life of the Church.[2] Once the liturgical action, which is really the action of Christ working in His Church for the sanctification and salvation of souls, is seen as a primarily human activity, the objective truth of doctrine and the cooperation with grace through obedience

2 *Sacrosanctum Concilium*, n. 10.

to discipline comes to be less and less respected in favor of a relativism centered upon man. Clearly, such a vision and praxis in the Church cannot last long because they lead to the corruption and destruction of the Christian life itself. In fact, the situation reached such a point after the Council that Pope Paul VI declared his perception that "from some crack the smoke of Satan has entered the temple of God."[3]

Faced with such a situation, there is only one way of going forward for the person of faith: the renewed appreciation of these neglected treasures, and persevering work aimed at restoring their rightful place in the Church. As Pope Benedict XVI wrote to the Bishops of the Latin rite of the Church, at the time of the promulgation of the Motu Proprio *Summorum Pontificum*:

> What earlier generations held as sacred, remains sacred and great for us too, and it cannot be all of a sudden entirely forbidden or even considered harmful. It behooves all of us to preserve the riches which have developed in the Church's faith and prayer, and to give them their proper place.[4]

It is important to identify and describe the severity of the situation, but we should not waste time trying to assign blame to someone for what happened. Instead, as Pope Benedict XVI has so brilliantly taught and shown, we must follow the path of reform, "of renewal in the continuity of the one subject-Church which the Lord has given to us."[5] With the celebration of Holy

3 *Insegnamenti di Paolo VI*, X:707.
4 *AAS* 99:798.
5 Address to the Roman Curia, December 22, 2005, *AAS* 98:46.

Mass again according to the *Vetus Ordo*, the organic unity of liturgical life in the Church is highlighted and strengthened.

At the same time, as Pope Benedict XVI and his predecessors have also urged us, we must effectively promote the study of the Latin language in general and especially in seminaries. The cultivation of Latin is an essential door to the more faithful and fuller appreciation of Tradition. Seminaries must again integrate into the curriculum of studies courses that lead to a good and effective knowledge of Latin. At the same time, the Church must offer to the faithful in general that repertoire of prayers and chants in Latin that constitute an important part of the patrimony of the Catholic faith. Without putting into doubt the goodness of Holy Mass in the vernacular, the faithful should regularly experience the celebration of Holy Mass in the language of the universal Church.

The work of restoration of the liturgy and of the study of Latin is exceptionally demanding. It will require years, and then care must also be taken not to fall once again into the "hermeneutic of discontinuity and rupture."[6] However, as I have experienced and continue to experience, there is a great new energy in the Church for true reform that fully respects her living Tradition. In my experience as a diocesan Bishop from 1995 to 2008, and in my visits to various parts of the world, I have met and still meet a substantial number of faithful, both older and younger, ready to sacrifice themselves for the liturgical renewal of the Church and to deepen their knowledge of the Latin language. I see that this readiness for a new evangelization, by means of the liturgical renewal and the renewed cultivation of the Latin language, is part of their Catholic faith, which

6   Ibid.

manifests itself in family life and in educational, charitable, and missionary works.

The present work — brief, yet abounding in content for our reflection — breathes this enthusiasm and energy. It inspires us to continue in the line that Pope Benedict XVI illustrated for us, and upon which he has set us forth and guided us. Fr. Roberto Spataro, a Salesian, basing himself on the sound pastoral practice of the Church, which is always firmly rooted in study and respect for doctrine, and on his masterful knowledge of Latin, offers us in a few pages words full of love for the Church, the Mystical Body of Christ, of pastoral charity, and of love for souls. With a series of conferences, given in various places in Italy and now collected in this work, he wanted to clarify the objective and lasting foundations of the interest in the classical form of the Roman rite and in the Latin language, in itself so well-adapted to serve the Church and, indeed, a key to the knowledge of the living Tradition of the Church. The texts of the conferences are alive with the enthusiasm and energy of a new evangelization. Reading them, one almost has the sensation of hearing them in person, because they are so profoundly grounded in the incomparable gift of the living Christ, transmitted to us in His Church and above all through the sacred liturgy.

Father Roberto Spataro does not speak of the *Vetus Ordo* of the Holy Mass as an historical artifact to be rescued, but as a living, sacramental vehicle by which Christ meets us, teaches us, and fills us with the grace of the Holy Spirit. In the same way, he does not see the Latin language as an historical relic to be preserved, but as a current and treasured tool for the communication of the faith through doctrine; for the response of faith by prayer and, above all, in divine worship and sound morals, in accord with the faith, promoted and safeguarded by discipline. All of the texts collected here are full of a true pastoral spirit. They express the heart of a faithful Salesian priest, of a true son of St John Bosco, and of a scholar inspired by a profound love for the living Church, for the many souls who thirst to know, love, and serve Christ, the only Savior of the World.

It only remains for me to express my profound gratitude to the author for the knowledge and love that he communicates to us in this little book, which truly constitutes the heart of a very large work. May the words of Father Roberto Spataro, full of so much pastoral charity, inspire each of us to commit ourselves to the true renewal of the sacred liturgy and of the study of the Latin language. May the gift of this paean be transformed into the gift of ourselves to a new evangelization, faithfully and generously working above all for the highest and most perfect expression of the Gospel: the Holy Mass, which is the Mystery of Faith, and for the cultivation of the Latin language as a perennial instrument of divine worship and of our whole life in Christ and in His Holy Church.

TRANSLATOR'S NOTE

The Foreword by Cardinal Burke and the first six chapters are translated from *Elogio della Messa Tridentina e del latino lingua della Chiesa* (Verona: Fede & Cultura, 2015). This English edition has benefited from the inclusion, as chapters 7 and 8, of thematically related lectures given by Fr. Spataro in 2017 and 2018.

INTRODUCTION

Patrick M. Owens

A T THE CONVENT OF DUNS SCO-
tus College in Southfield, Michigan, the sun
had just begun to set as the young Franciscan
novices stood in choir for Vespers. Suddenly,
furtive glances and stifled chuckles interrupted
the customary solemnity of the chapel as the verse "Et percussit
inimicos suos in posteriora" (Ps 77:66) was sung. The surprised
novices understood the verse as "And [the Lord] struck His
enemies in their backsides."

It was 1948, and the Order of Friars Minor had recently
returned to the Vulgate translation of the Psalms after an inaus-
picious experiment with the Bea Psalter. These twenty-three
friars, who had been Franciscans for less than two years, had
grown familiar with the Pian version of the same verse, "Et
percussit a tergo inimicos suos" (And [the Lord] struck His
enemies from their back).

All these novices had studied Latin for at least four years
before their simple profession. In the Franciscan minor seminaries — basically their equivalent of high school — students had
five hours of Latin classes and at least as many hours of liturgy
in Latin each week. During novitiate there were no formal academic classes; rather, it was a time devoted to formation and
discernment. As such, they were obliged to recite the entire
Divine Office in choir, attend Mass daily, and listen to seminars
on the Order's Rule, all of which were in Latin and accounted
for at least four hours each day. Latin was not a *foreign* language;

it was the language of the Church. The novices did not study it at a distance; they *lived* it. Having such familiarity with the language, it was not surprising that the novices would hear the changed words of the Psalm and immediately attribute to *posteriora* its ridiculous common meaning. They were not translating the Latin. They were understanding it.

Another example of this integration of Latin into the rhythms of religious life also occurred at a seminary. Fr. Reginald Foster, OCD, once recalled that in 1954 at the minor seminary in Peterborough, New Hampshire, the novice-master admonished a Carmelite novice to wash off his grease-laden hands. In response the novice raised his blacked hands to his superior and quipped, "Nigra sum sed formosa," a clever reference to a Vespers antiphon taken from the Canticle of Canticles: "I am black, but beautiful" (Cant 1:4). The novice-master chuckled, and the novice was able to escape further rebuke.

The deep and instinctive familiarity with Latin illustrated by these stories resulted from a comprehensive and immersive education in the language. Kenneth Baker, SJ, recounts that when he was a Jesuit seminarian in the 1950s, not only were all the seminary classes taught in Latin and from Latin textbooks, but the annual oral examinations were also conducted in Latin. All recreation time in novitiate was in Latin — meaning that for much of the day, novices were expected either to speak Latin or not to speak at all. Men who intended to enter the Order without knowing Latin were required to complete a two-year Juniorate, which helped them bridge the gap. By the time of ordination, most Jesuits with such a background had read a great part of the Classics and of the Church Fathers in the original and could write and speak Latin. The Jesuit education was, in fact, a liberal arts curriculum with an emphasis on the Classics.

Nevertheless, Latin was not the exclusive province of priests and religious. Within living memory, Catholic school children in both Europe and America learned their Latin prayers and grammar. Boys as young as eight years old could recite from memory the prayers at the foot of the altar. Even children (girls perhaps to a lesser extent) from working class families could be expected to know the Mass and to have read some Vergil and Caesar by age fourteen. Before the last century, by the age of sixteen, a diligent though unexceptional student from a well-off family would have attained a level of mastery in Latin that would surpass that of many current graduate students of the Classics.

To be sure, Latin was larger than the schoolroom or the choir. The language that had served the Western world as a lingua franca for nearly two millennia was still the official language of the Church's hierarchy, prayer, and diplomacy. Beyond sheer formalities, it fulfilled a genuine need in the Church even into the 20th century: Latin was the actual mode of international communication between priests and scholars. Catholics were not studying Latin merely as a scholastic exercise, but rather for the sake of acquiring their venerable tradition and laying foundations for an enduring intellectual and spiritual culture.

CHURCH LATIN: A MANY-SIDED REALITY

The *Acta Apostolicae Sedis* (AAS) is only one typical example of the way clergy and laity alike used Latin as a genuine means of communication in the last century. As the official monthly gazette of the Catholic Church, it contained all the news that Rome saw fit to print. The AAS brought news of ecclesial appointments, the contents and digest version of encyclical letters, and the decisions of Roman congregations in reply to *dubia*. When Catholics were uncertain about the validity of a certain sect's sacraments, a particularly thorny annulment petition, whether they might enjoy a relaxation of fasting or abstinence on some account, or how to recognize a newly canonized saint in the recitation of the Divine Office, for these and numerous other queries, there was found in the AAS a repository of current responses and practical assistance of which the faithful could avail themselves. The laws contained in the AAS were considered promulgated as soon as they were published, leaving no time for translations into various languages.

With rare exceptions, AAS was published entirely in Latin, a practice that on account of the gravity of the subject matters and the international audience was never seriously questioned. In fact, AAS was only the latest iteration (having been preceded by the *Acta Sanctae Sedis* and the *Acta et Decreta*) of expansive international publishing for the benefit and governance of hundreds of millions of faithful. In the minds of the authors, the linguistic continuity of these publications ensured that they would be accessible to Catholics of any future generation. In 1940 a Catholic with little more than a high school degree could make sense of a literary corpus ranging from this month's edition of the *Acta Apostolicae Sedis* back to the *Acta Martyrum Scillitanorum* (the account of the Scillitan Martyrs from A D 180). This connection with an immutable language meant that modern people were able to be in dialogue with past generations using the same literary models, technical terminology, and allusions to Scripture or liturgy. From the Vatican cloister to the high schools of Brooklyn, Catholics prayed, studied, travelled, litigated, and even joked in Latin *ut sint unum*.

But arguably the strongest thread holding this long fiber of Latin culture together across the centuries was the Latin liturgy. By virtue of its being the central and universal prayer of the Church, the Divine Office is the first contact for both clergy and faithful with the sublime liturgical idiom of the West. Furthermore, when the faithful pray the Divine Office, the prayer of the individual joins with that of the diocese and of the universal Church, in an act that transcends temporal and spatial boundaries. Though consisting principally of Psalms, the Divine Office also contains many of the Church's most elaborate orations, petitions, and ancient homilies. The august poetry of the psalter and meticulous diction of orations provide the faithful with a common voice and universal language into which the Franciscan novices of Duns Scotus College and countless previous generations around the world assimilated their prayer. Because Latin was an essential feature of this communal liturgy, experienced by all Catholics, the liturgy ensured in turn that Latin remained an integral part of Catholics' cultural memory.

Arguably one of the most important reasons that Latin education must be kept alive in the Church is to retain access to this communal experience of liturgy. Why? Because this liturgy is the repository of the Catholic tradition.

It is education that conserves and transmits the experience and wisdom of the previous generations so that such a cultural memory, identity, and common parlance can be forged and strengthened. Indeed, for most of human history, this inculturation has been a primary purpose of education. Language encapsulates the culture and the history of a society. Those elements are passed to the successive generations through the language so that future generations may benefit from the sufferings and discoveries of their forebears and enjoy the comfort of participation in a transcendent community that reaches back through the ages. Rightly conceived, culture is the conscious ideal of human perfection and the habitual vision of greatness. In the case of Catholic culture, this community originates with the Apostles and Our Lord Himself. The language that provides the Divine Office with its poetic freedom and simultaneously constrains the prose to prescriptive ancient norms carries in its rich history an immense treasure of thought and feeling from both pre-Christian and Apostolic times. For the better part of two thousand years, it has provided the Church with a language of worship, an intellectual clarity, and a mark of catholicity.

Catholic culture — the *sensus fidelium* — is replete with ideas about fasting and feasting, domestic devotions, processions and pilgrimages, all expressed in one unifying idiom of Latin. But culture cannot be infused; it must be taught, absorbed, and lived. And although the accoutrements of Catholic culture are only ancillary to the Sacraments, they nonetheless furnish an integral part of the identity of the Roman Church and therefore of its members. This core identity of the Church is what is at stake in the current controversies regarding the role of Latin.

A BRIEF HISTORY OF LATIN IN THE CHURCH

Comparing millennia of a shared Catholic linguistic inheritance to the current condition of Latin leads inevitably to one question: how did it happen that such an ancient language fell, seemingly so suddenly, into disuse and even ignominy? The common and clichéd answer is "Vatican II," but such a response is a vast oversimplification, one that ignores the more long-term transformations in Western culture and in Latin pedagogy that have led us to our present unhappy situation. Of course, the space of a book's introduction does not permit an extensive history of the use of Latin in the Church. A brief summary, however, is in order, discussing the reasons for Latin's decline in the modern period, and pointing out places where a contemporary recovery of authentic pedagogy is currently taking place. It is against this backdrop that Fr. Spataro's contribution can be fully appreciated.

The use of Latin in the Church dates as far back as Pentecost itself.[1] Although the Western liturgical transition from Greek to Latin happened gradually, the seat of the Church in Rome allowed for a sort of second, though less miraculous, Pentecost: the fact that, through Latin, all the peoples of Europe could hear the Gospel in a common tongue. The use of Latin in the administration of the Empire and the early translations of Gospels aided the spread of the faith, much as did the great Roman system of roads, but the vernacular dialect of bureaucrats and merchants was not the model for Latin in the Church. In fact, two of the greatest Latin minds of the early Church, Saints Augustine and Jerome, found the language of Sacred Scripture to be "shameful" and "horrible" respectively.[2] Over time, through the contributions of the Latin Fathers and the common repository of formal prayers, the marriage of the idiom of Latin Gospel translations and the rhetorical flourish of Roman oratory gave birth to a recognizable Christian idiom.[3] From early on, the power and prestige of Rome and its church pulled into its orbit other churches, over which it exerted considerable influence.[4]

---

1   Cf. Acts 2:10.

2   Cf. St. Augustine, *Confessiones* 3.5.9, and St. Jerome, *Epistulae* XXII.30.

3   Christian or Vulgar Latin has been the object of intense scholarly work over the past half-century by scholars like József Herman, Christine Mohrmann, Michael Lang, and Roger Wright.

4   This phenomenon is most recognizable in the letters of St. Clement as well as in St. Ambrose's deference to the Roman liturgy.

Although Latin was the vernacular of Rome, the language of the Roman church's worship was always a sacred tongue. There is nothing quotidian about the rhythm and diction of the Roman Canon, and the vocabulary and impressive cadence of the Vulgate Psalter undeniably evoke grandeur. The Church Fathers of the West defended the faith and spread the Gospel in a number of registers above the unhewn language of the translations of Sacred Scripture. Most particularly, they introduced the technical terminology of Christian Latin, which they themselves coined or borrowed from Greek. The elevated register of Christian Latin ultimately replaced Greek in the sacred rites of the West, in part because it was more palatable to the educated Roman elite than Greek or vulgar Latin. The evangelization of the Roman cultural aristocracy was the primary impetus behind the development of Rome's own liturgical idiom.

We have already seen the pride of place given to the Latin language at the founding of the Church. Years later the collapse of the Roman Empire did not mean the collapse of Latin. Instead, as civil society floundered, Latin became an even greater unifying force across Europe, amidst the growing ethnic diversity of the Church's members and subjects. The establishment of Christendom solidified Latin not only in Church administration, but also in trade, politics, international diplomacy, and universities. Nor did the emergence of national languages displace Latin. It remained the language of learning for centuries after the spread of vernacular literature. After the watershed moment for vernacular literature at the start of the fourteenth century when Dante composed his *Divine Comedy*, scholars and artists of every stripe like Petrarch, Kepler, Galileo, Newton, Leibniz, and even Nietzsche continued to write principal works in Latin. The use of Latin was so common up through the nineteenth century as to be taken for granted throughout Europe and its colonies. Until that time, there was no interval of time when Latin was not spoken in universities and throughout the Church. For most of the modern period, a graduate student of any field would have been embarrassed to submit a dissertation that was not in Latin. Even a vicar or an auxiliary bishop could write in Latin expeditiously to his superior about any urgent need, and any bishop or cardinal was reasonably expected to be more or less extemporaneously conversant in the language of the Church, as evidenced by the extensive correspondence between them and the Vatican during the preparatory period before the Second Vatican Council.

Latin was especially important for countries whose national languages were either too diverse or too different from the rest of Europe for easy communication. In Hungary, the national language remained Latin until the nineteenth century. It was the language of politics, administration, education, and the judiciary. Orations and public debates at every level were held in Latin. More than just an official language, Latin was also the language of the everyday communication of society. Of course, not every Hungarian was an eloquent speaker, and language proficiency was dependent upon one's level of education. Nevertheless, after the elementary schools, which were conducted mostly in Hungarian, secondary school courses were taught in Latin. Throughout the eighteenth and nineteenth centuries western European travelers who had visited Hungary remarked with awe that the Latin language was in daily use by a variety of people, not only the nobility and the clergy, but oftentimes even simple folk. Latin represented for Hungarians a bond with the glorious past of the Kingdom, a direct link with classical antiquity, an intellectual connection with Western culture, and a token of national unity, which was especially critical for an empire that was comprised of Croatians, Germans, Serbs, Slovaks, and Turks, all of whom had their own native languages.[5] In this way, Hungary's use of Latin mirrored that of the Church.

The Church's adherence to this common practice of utilizing Latin as a lingua franca should not be surprising. Languages are intrinsically bound to cultures, and Latin for nearly two-thousand years had been the language not only of Catholic culture in the West but of Western culture itself. It is for this reason that the Church took pains to keep alive the tradition of active Latin. Catholic intellectuals knew well that since Latin was the vehicle of culture, a superficial familiarity would not be sufficient. To ensure the ability to engage with past sources and contemporary intellectuals as well as to protect the transference of Catholic culture to subsequent generations, active language use is essential. Catholic leaders, therefore, took pains to master the Catholic language not only passively through extensive reading and public lectures, but also actively by developing the ability to communicate effectively and rhetorically in written and extemporaneous spoken exchanges. This tradition persisted into modern times, producing the outstanding Catholic scholars, many of them priests and bishops, who distinguished themselves during the first half of the twentieth century. This same tradition allowed for elegant orations and spirited debates in Latin among over 2,000 bishops and religious superiors at the Second Vatican Council, where the comparatively small number of prelates incapable of extemporaneous Latin conversation

5   Cf. Hugh F. Graham, "Latin in Hungary," *The Classical Journal* 63, no. 4 (1968): 163–65; Ármin Vámbéry, *Arminius Vambéry: His Life and Adventures* (London: Fisher Unwin, 1884), 5; Thomas Capek, *The Slovaks of Hungary* (New York: Knickerbocker Press, 1906), 176–80.

enjoyed personal translators. If Latin's position, even as late as the time of Vatican II, appeared so solid, what had been the hidden fault lines that led to such a seemingly abrupt fissure between past and present?

CAUSES OF DIMINISHMENT

In truth, several trends contributed to the crisis we face in Latin today, and all have roots long before the Second Vatican Council.

Beginning as early as the Hundred Years' War, European countries used French rather than Latin for secular diplomatic purposes. When the salons of France became intellectual incubators of the Enlightenment, French became more widely accepted in academic circles as well. The Enlightenment thinkers themselves were, generally speaking, hostile to tradition and the supremacy of the Church, and, by extension, to Latin. The French Revolution fomented nationalistic identity and cemented the divorce of France from the Catholic Church. From then on, national patriotism eclipsed Catholic identity across much of former Christendom: Catholics in Europe or America increasingly experienced their faith as merely one part of their identity, in competition with nationality, political party affiliation, and other elements of modern life. As such, national languages and regional dialects took precedence over what was increasingly seen as the vestiges of ancient inscriptions and an esoteric language of the Church. As decades passed, French continued to overtake Latin in the courts and universities of Europe. A third language did not become a prominent competitor in diplomacy until perhaps the signing of the Treaty of Versailles, when the British Empire and ascendant America had a lasting impact on the new age of diplomacy.

By the nineteenth century across Europe and the Americas, Latin had lost much of its prestige outside the Church: it no longer had a practical application as a medium for trade or diplomacy and had lost its grip on the universities. Although academicians at the University of Paris (and a negligible number of other European universities) continued to compose and defend their dissertations in Latin into the 1920s, over the course of the nineteenth century, Latin was gradually displaced by the vernacular languages in one of its oldest and most exalted strongholds: academia. Although the study of Latin was certainly not abolished, any pretense of Latin as a requirement in the university systems for *all* fields of study had largely atrophied into a mere formality. Once universities lifted even the formal requirement of Latin for advanced studies, students outside of the Classics were no longer under any obligation to master Latin in order to understand lectures, write papers, or defend their theses. As a consequence, the methods for teaching and learning Latin radically shifted, since it was no longer viewed as the prestigious central language but as an anemic relic. Once Latin lost its place as the prestigious lingua franca of the academy, the career of Latin as a living language was finished.

The diminished arenas in which Latin communication was appropriate brought about reconsideration of the goals of classical training and education. This shift in educational objectives has grown gradually from as early as the Protestant Reformation. Although the principal thinkers of early Protestantism were accomplished and learned men, many Protestants rejected the use of Latin either inside or outside of worship. Both Calvin and Luther advocated for a classical education, but since their church was no longer centered in

Rome, their Bible was no longer the Vulgate, and their worship no longer admitted Latin,[6] the ability to write and speak the language was seen as non-essential. It was thus sufficient for school children to learn the rudiments of grammar and how to read some Latin without requiring fluency or compositional proficiency.

THE HUMANIST METHOD

It is worth asking here, what methods have been historically used for teaching Latin? Many today would imagine Latin classrooms of yesteryear as being very similar to their own, wherein students were charged to master charts of forms and syntactical rules with brief examples until, in the second year, they read Caesar's *Gallic Wars*.

Yet, contrary to popular belief, this method, often called the grammar-translation method, is a fairly recent development in the teaching of classical languages. In fact, the grammar-translation method does not date back much beyond the nineteenth century, when Latin as an academic language had already begun its decline. This method relies on a decontextualization of Latin grammar and syntax from literature. Such a utilitarian approach gained wide acceptance in the last two centuries and diverged dramatically from the traditional Catholic Humanist method of teaching Latin as a spoken and written language. Indeed, the system of instruction that was traditionally used in the schools of Catholic and Protestant Humanists for centuries was entirely

6 The Lutheran liturgy in certain areas retained pre-Reformation prayers in their original languages (e.g., the Kyrie in Greek or the Gloria in Latin), which explains why we have a number of such Mass settings by the greatest of Lutheran composers, Johann Sebastian Bach. Nevertheless, the vast majority of Lutheran vocal music was in German.

different from the tiresome pedantry that characterizes much of the popular image of Latin learning. The active method never completely disappeared, however, and pedagogues have attempted to restore it, with varying success.

What was the Catholic Humanist tradition? The Humanists criticized the grammarians of the Late Middle Ages who had subordinated literary pursuits to speculative investigations. At the time, the accepted wisdom was that the Latin of classical authors had always been an artificial language created by the learned elite as a lingua franca for Western culture. But the re-vernacularization of Latin had had quite a different outcome: the language recognized as the universal lingua franca splintered. As Latin became less constrained by grammatical rules or classical precedents, the language of philosophy and theology developed its own technical dialect, and the language of law and business became its own jargon as well, heavily influenced by vernacular borrowings.

Despite the heroic work accomplished by the Carolingians in conserving ancient and Patristic sources, by the 12th century renaissance the re-introduction of Aristotle through translations and the new scholastic movement overwhelmed Latin literature with its own scholastic dialect. It was not only in this specialized province that Latin suffered a diminution in its universality; regional variations arose quite separate from the modern languages.[7] At its nadir the dialects lost mutual intelligibility, and some Scholastic writers struggled to make sense of stylized Latin from antiquity. On the eve of the Renaissance, Petrarch was chided at the French court for using Classical Latin, which

---

7 Frank A. C. Rigg, "Medieval Latin Philology," in *Medieval Latin* (Washington, DC: Catholic University of America Press, 1996), 74–76.

those present could not understand, rather than a variety of quotidian Latin.[8]

The Humanists advocated a return to the original sources of ancient learning. After rediscovering lost works of Cicero and Livy, Petrarch reintroduced classical Latinity into the court of the Holy Roman Empire. Subsequent Humanists brought about a revolution in teaching methods that reinvigorated the Latin tradition though the cultivation of the best authors and the pruning of barbaric innovations. Thus, they were directly responsible for the language's resurgence and four more centuries of its life. Thanks to the efforts of the Humanists, Latin was able to reestablish its continuity with the most prominent authors and standards of the past, so that Latinists throughout Europe were again in real dialogue with the greatest of both contemporary Europe and the ancient world. This second wind, which is often identified as Neo-Latin, allowed writers of Latin to record and transmit the incredible innovations and numerous transformations of culture, including the scientific revolution of the sixteenth and seventeenth centuries, across Europe and the New World.

Humanist educators composed very short grammars as the basic introduction to the language. After learning just the essential declensions and regular conjugations, students passed immediately to active exercises: learning vocabulary divided by themes, greetings, short conversations, small compositions, and exercises imitating the letters of ancient authors. The *colloquia* in particular had such a widespread popularity that the *colloquium* soon became a literary genre all to itself, which was then expanded and improved by Erasmus and many others.

8 *Rerum memorandarum libri*, ed. Giuseppe Billanovich, Edizione nazionale delle opere di Francesco Petrarca, 5 (Florence: Sansoni, 1945), 40, 1.37.9.

Within the *colloquia*, there is a studied and regular repetition of words to aid students in their memory of vocabulary and syntax. The tradition of the *colloquia* was rooted in an ancient teaching tradition, dating back to the *Hermeneumata* of the third century, whose influence was in various ways continued until at least the eleventh century.

THE ENLIGHTENMENT'S INFLUENCE

Despite the revival of Latin under the Humanists, the influence of Enlightenment philosophies and the scientific method on eighteenth-century educators resulted in a tendency to place a premium on systematic and structural approaches to language learning. The grammar-translation method is ostensibly more systematic and structuralist than the Humanists' method insofar as it proceeds from grammatical elements to syntactical structures and reinforces an anatomical hermeneutic. It also encourages the student to view the Latin sentence as something to be deconstructed rather than read.

This pseudo-scientific approach led to the next trend threatening authentic Latin study. By the early twentieth century, educational reformers in Germany, Britain, Italy, and the United States began promoting the study of classical languages as a proxy for logic, attention to detail, and a certain kind of mental gymnastics: skills that would have broader application to other fields of study outside of the Classics, making them more "practical."[9] According to this view, whether students

9 This method aims to enable students "to benefit from the mental discipline and intellectual development that result from foreign language study." See *Approaches and Methods in Language Teaching*, 3rd ed., ed. Jack C. Richards and Theodore S. Rodgers (Cambridge: Cambridge University Press, 2001), 3–5.

learned Latin idiom was of secondary concern; the motivation for studying classical languages was derived from a goal external to their literary and cultural heritage. Latin began to be regarded as a tool by which students could develop analytical faculties, a patience for mental work, and obedience to rational rules. These metalinguistic skills, conceptual tools, and systematic capacities were often considered transferable to the mathematical disciplines. While these are certainly laudable educational goals, educators dedicated to this new grammar-translation method made Latin a means to an end rather than a central facet of the liberal arts. This resulted in a depreciation of the study of Latin for its own sake, a diminished mastery of Latin idiom, and a separation of the study of Latin from literary delights.[10]

Finally, the Enlightenment's reaction against the ecclesial domain, along with growing nationalist sentiments, cultivated a perspective that criticized traditional active pedagogy as being too closely aligned with the Church. The Enlightenment's characteristic fascination with novelty motivated even the rejection of educational models rooted in antiquity on account of their ecclesiastical affiliations. By the eighteenth century much of Latin language education had devolved into a decadent parroting of Latin formulae. As a result, Latinists faced a mounting reaction against the Classics for seeming devoid of the *esprit* of the modern age and out of touch with the salons.

---

10 "The method adopted in Italian schools for the instruction of classical languages is the most difficult and least profitable; it confers little of the knowledge of the language, and less of the knowledge of the literary spirit." *M. P. I., Commissione reale per l'ordinamento degli studi secondari in Italia* (Rome, 1909), cited in G. Pittàno, *Didattica del latino* (Milan: B. Mondadori, 1978), 35.

Until the middle of the seventeenth century, the majority of books were published in Latin. But within a century, the percentage of books published in other languages, principally French, increased throughout Europe.[11] As authors of the period turned away from Latin and towards vernacular languages, the market embraced the change in order to maximize their readership. Educators then reconsidered the emphasis placed on Latin within the school curricula. Many of the luminaries of the Enlightenment, including Diderot, Rousseau, and Voltaire, reacted against contemporary pedagogies as sterile and formalistic. The reformers lacked the historical perspective to distinguish between the formalistic approach that was distorting and stifling the Humanistic methods and the authentic Humanistic system that was founded on ancient and early medieval models and approached the Classics holistically. The Enlightenment educational reforms largely regarded the formalistic approach as inseparable from the study of the Classics, and, therefore, they contemned the entire field of study as superfluous.[12]

NEW PHILOLOGY

Excitement over new philological discoveries struck another blow against authentic Latin education. After William Jones's discovery that Latin, Greek, and Sanskrit had a common ancestor received broad acceptance, it opened up entirely new areas

11   Robert Darnton, *The Literary Underground of the Old Regime* (Cambridge, MA: Harvard University Press, 1982).

12   For a treatment of this see Georg Bollenbeck, *Bildung und Kultur: Glanz und Elend eines deutschen Deutungsmusters* (Frankfurt: Insel, 1994), and Georges Snyders, *La pédagogie en France aux XVIIe et XVIIIe siècles* (Paris: Presses Universitaires des Francs, 1964).

of research in the field of linguistics. The German school of philology began to value lines of inquiry that were more linguistic than classical in nature. These advances in the scientific knowledge of the classical languages, which allowed for a deeper study both of their points of intersection and of previously impenetrable etymologies, steadily outstripped the seemingly antiquated holistic appreciation of Latin literature. This led to hyperspecialization even within the field of Classics — so much so that a large part of the field of classical philology, which was once concerned with classical literature, began exclusively to pursue questions of comparative or historical linguistics and the new Lachmannian approaches to textual criticism, which placed the greatest importance on uncovering the original text from antiquity.

The extension of philological erudition and grammatical, morphological, and syntactic analysis beyond the knowledge and needs proper to secondary school resulted in exactly the opposite of what was intended: students actually developed a weaker mastery *of* the classical languages as they learned more *about* them. The philological word or even morpheme became the main objective of instruction. This overemphasis did not produce classically literate students but German parakeets. Language lessons became in effect another form of mental gymnastics, whereby the students became practiced in learning trivia devoid of practical application, literary context, or cultural significance.[13]

---

13 "Reading no longer excites any emotion in the hearts of students because the textbooks recall only the Schultz and the Madvig [erudite philologists], and never evoke ancient life." *Relazioni sull'insegnamento del latino nella scuola media*, in G. Pascoli, *Prose* (Milan: Mondadori, 1946), 1:607.

THE HUMANISTS' METHOD RESURGENT

In 1902, however, a new and promising wave of Latin pedagogy began, when William Henry Denham Rouse, a scholar of the Classics and founder of the Loeb Classical Library, left Cambridge University. Rouse was worried about the precipitous drop in the skills of the university students that he was encountering there. He ascribed this decrease in Latin and Greek ability to the introduction of new "devastating methods" of writing: "The method currently in use is not older than the nineteenth century. It is the son of German scholarship, which attempts to learn everything about one thing rather than the thing in itself."[14]

Rouse exposed the evils he saw in the German grammar-translation method and proposed a remedy. He took over the Perse School, which was on the brink of bankruptcy, and quickly hired several excellent teachers.[15] Together they wrote books on the theory and practice of teaching classical languages with active pedagogy, which they called the Direct Method. What they proposed was, in fact, a modified version of the Catholic Humanist tradition of treating Latin more like a natural language and using it in an immersive environment. Rouse's students learned Latin by progressing from very simple expressions to more complicated dialogues, even discussing in Latin what they read or saw. Despite Rouse's formidable erudition, his instruction style bore little resemblance to the dry and arcane philological scholarship of his contemporaries. Instead,

14 W. H. D. Rouse and R. B. Appleton, *Latin on the Direct Method* (London: University of London, 1925).

15 W. H. D. Rouse, *Scenes from Sixth Form Life* (Oxford: Blackwell, 1935); Christopher Stray, *The Living Word: W. H. D. Rouse and the Crisis of Classics in Edwardian England* (Bristol Classical Press, 1992).

he presented his students with simple texts and an entertaining immersive environment, in just the same way that many of the greatest Humanists learned and taught Latin and Greek.

Rouse's experimental approach was so successful that the Board of Education financed the school to support the initiative and research the scalability of the project. Rouse and the Perse School's reputation spread far and wide; in 1912 Prof. Gonzalez Lodge invited Rouse to give a Direct Method summer school at Columbia University. By 1915, Rouse and his colleagues had published several teaching guides and textbooks for use with the Direct Method.[16] At the same time, many teachers from around Great Britain and Europe visited the Perse School to see how Rouse's actual classroom compared with the reports. Educators were so interested in the success of the Perse School that Rouse began conducting further summer schools in which instructors could learn the techniques of the Direct Method and improve their ability to speak Latin (and Greek). Through these summer schools reform-minded educators created materials and discussed plans of bringing the Direct Method to other schools around the world.

The opening of hostilities in Europe prevented further progress, however, and England's entrance into the war in the summer of 1914 marked the end of Rouse's reform. Many of his most skilled colleagues perished in the Great War, which destroyed the younger generation of teachers, leaving mostly older teachers who were less interested in Rouse's experimental

16 W. H. S. Jones of St Catharine's College published his *First Latin Book* in 1907. Oxford University Press published Rouse's series of texts under the series title *Lingua Latina* from 1912 to 1931. Appleton published his collection of original plays, *Perse Latin Plays*, in 1913 and his introductory textbook *Initium* in 1916.

approaches. After the war, Rouse and others attempted to regain some lost ground. Rouse's pedagogy was undeniably effective, but it made very heavy demands on the teacher, who needed to be not only proficient in the Classics but also a fluent extemporaneous speaker and capable of motivating students. Unfortunately, very few were up to the task. Rouse's reform of the British schools was essentially stillborn. The Direct Method textbooks gradually went out of print. The grammar-translation method remained dominant and is perhaps partially to blame for the abolition of compulsory Latin at Oxbridge and elsewhere in the 1960s.

Later in the twentieth century, a similar project was envisioned by the Danish scholar, Hans Henning Ørberg. Ørberg, who had been a specialist at the Nature Method Institute, a center for research in second language acquisition in Copenhagen, hoped to bring the fruit of his research to bear upon Latin. From 1955 to 1983 he worked on a natural approach to Latin, using highly contextual induction and textual immersion. Ørberg drew inspiration from the success that Rouse had enjoyed, but identified some of his shortcomings. In the final editions of Ørberg's monumental work *Familia Rōmāna,* he brought together both contemporary research and the frequency lists of vocabulary and morphology found in the most read classical authors. In this way the text, which is based around a compelling story of a Roman family, introduces the learner to the most frequent words and explains them entirely in Latin. Ørberg's approach lifted much of the burden off of the teacher by creating marginal notes that conveyed meaning through illustration or description in Latin. The carefully designed story, copious Latin annotations, and judiciously chosen vocabulary free the instructor from the need to supplement from his own internal resources, thus making smaller demands upon him. In many ways, this work is the completion of Rouse's plan and a direct descendant of the Catholic Humanist school of Latin pedagogy.

Although these two prominent reformers and educators who promoted the Catholic-Humanist tradition of Latin education in the last century were neither Catholic nor lived in Catholic countries, Latin was not entirely abandoned in Rome. Fr. Reginald Foster, an American Carmelite who served three popes as a Vatican Latinist, is the most famous modern Latin speaker in the Anglophone world. Fr. Foster came to Rome in 1960 where he worked in the Latin Letters Office until his retirement in 2009. He gained notoriety through the courses he taught during the academic year at the Gregorianum and during the summer months at his monastery. Fr. Foster insisted on using only "real Latin," which he excerpted from texts of all periods. He rejected the Latinity of school books as subpar and stilted. At the same time, he encouraged oral facility in the language and for decades was widely regarded as the most able Latin speaker in the world. Fr. Foster's promotion of a return to original sources, use of spoken Latin, and overall pedagogical style galvanized a vibrant movement among contemporary American Latinists.

Two institutions in Rome have attempted to fill the void created by Fr. Foster's retirement from active teaching. In 2010, Dr. Luigi Miraglia moved his *Accademia Vivarium Novum* from a small town outside of Naples to Rome. The *Vivarium* is an international residential institution for the study of Classics and Renaissance literature; it is unique in that all instruction and the entirety of the school's community life takes place in Latin. In many ways, the *Accademia* is the ideal eighteenth-century Jesuit Juniorate, except that it is essentially a secular institution.

In 1964, Paul VI established the *Institutum Altioris Latinitatis* at the Salesian Pontifical Institute to provide a center for the study of Latin and the Classics in Rome. Over the past half-century, the *Institutum* has maintained a great deal of autonomy from the norms of other Pontifical institutes. Here some of the most competent Latinists in the Church teach courses entirely in Latin, and their students routinely defend theses and dissertations in Latin. Despite the ignorance and antipathy that many members of the Church hierarchy often demonstrate toward the official language of the Church, the *Institutum* has persevered, publishing an astonishing volume of erudite research and cultivating an internationally recognized faculty. The recent success of the *Institutum Altioris Latinitatis* — due in part to the vision and direction provided by Fr. Roberto Spataro — led Benedict XVI to appoint Fr. Spataro as the secretary of the *Pontificia Academia Latinitatis* in 2012. There Fr. Spataro supports many initiatives to encourage the study, use, and promotion of Latin throughout the Catholic Church. The following book is but one example of Fr. Spataro's zeal for the language and literature of the Church, love of the Latin liturgy, and his understanding of the critical importance of protecting Latin's historical role as a conduit for Catholic culture.

The Rediscovery of the Traditional Liturgy after *Summorum Pontificum*

REASONS TO KNOW AND LOVE THE TRIDENTINE MASS[†]

Honored ladies, distinguished gentlemen, dear friends,

IT IS AN HONOR TO SPEAK THIS EVE-
ning before an audience of sincere and fervent believers
who share with me the same love for the Tridentine
Mass and—I am sure—veneration for the Pope Emeritus Benedict XVI, who with his Motu Proprio *Summorum Pontificum* has given back to the Church the Missal
of 1962, that treasure house of doctrine and piety. I am very
grateful to everyone present and to those whose great efforts
have promoted this timely initiative in Verona, a city ennobled
by its Christian tradition and symbolically exalted by the episode
of the Veronese Easter.[1]

I propose a series of reflections born partly from study and

---

1 Beginning on the morning of April 17, 1797, the second day of
Easter, the people of Verona revolted against French occupying forces
while Napoleon was fighting in Austria. The Veronese defeated over a
thousand soldiers in the first hour of fighting. The revolt ended on April
25, 1797, when the town was encircled and captured by 15,000 soldiers.

† A LECTURE GIVEN IN VERONA, MARCH 2014.

partly, I might say especially, from experience. The title of this conference makes specific reference to the rediscovery of the liturgy after the publication of *Summorum Pontificum*. This rediscovery among faithful and priests and in a consistent and significant percentage of youth and middle-aged people is an evident fact in many geographical areas. As far as I know, there are no official statistics. In any case, to rely on numbers betrays a certain pride and presumption. Nevertheless, the fact has been documented. It is sufficient to visit internet sites and blogs that publish news relating to the celebration of the liturgy according to the extraordinary form of the Roman rite to become aware of the phenomenon. I would like to propose three considerations.

First of all, the extraordinary form of the Roman rite interests a growing number of faithful who constitute, among the whole number of practicing Catholics, an extremely tiny minority, but one clearly endowed with very strong motivations, energetic in action, and at times disposed to militate for their cause. These are a few of the characteristics of what is called a "creative minority," a category studied by A. Toynbee and later applied by then Cardinal Ratzinger to the re-evangelization of secularized Europe. When we consider the history of the Church, we notice that creative minorities have effectively regenerated ecclesial life and brought a beneficent influence to all of society in moments of profound and extensive crisis of values and customs. We think, for example, of the first generations of Cluniac monks, protagonists in a 10th-century liturgical movement described thus by Benedict XVI:

> We want to indicate the central role the liturgy
> should occupy in the Christian life. The Cluniac
> monks dedicated themselves with love and great care

to the celebration of the liturgical Hours, to singing the Psalms, to devout and solemn processions, and above all, to the celebration of the Holy Mass. They fostered sacred music; they desired art and architecture to contribute to the beauty and solemnity of the rites; they enriched the liturgical calendar with special celebrations as, for example, the Commemoration of the Faithful Departed at the beginning of November; they augmented the cult of the Blessed Virgin Mary.[2]

Thanks to the monastic movement of Cluny, the people of Europe were woven into a robust ethical and spiritual fabric.

In second place, minorities tend to foster and defend their identity, contributing to a deeper and stronger appropriation of the traits that define their identity. For this reason, only a few years after the birth of the *Summorum Pontificum* movement, the faithful and communities that celebrate according to the Missal of 1962 are in a phase of maturation. Have not many of us had this experience? The liturgical formation we seek to obtain with others, the discovery of the duties of our spiritual life, and even the very process of organizing these celebrations, are showing us that the traditional liturgy creates a style of Christian life *tout court*.

Finally, I cannot pass over the fact that the minorities who have adopted the extraordinary form of the Roman rite do not always encounter understanding, despite the authoritative encouragement offered by the Motu Proprio. This fact is also, I think, of some importance. The history of the Church

---

2 Benedict XVI, "The Cluniac Reform," General Audience, November 11, 2009.

shows this constant law: the works of God are entrusted to a few. Especially in the beginning, they are resisted. Usually those who pose obstacles are brothers in the faith, acting with good intentions. God is served even in this mysterious dynamism of purification and consolidation.

Often people have asked us why we love the Tridentine Mass, and we have given them the reasons that seem important to us! Imagining an ideal interlocutor, a believer like us who wonders what value a "Latin Mass" could have, officiated by a priest who "turns his back" on the faithful, I would like to submit the following to your diligent attention. The reasons are five.

A LITURGY THAT LIFTS OUR HEARTS TO GOD

I would like to begin with the magisterium of Pope Francis. Indeed, besides the objective datum of the authority of the Supreme Pastor, this approach almost certainly guarantees benevolence in our ideal interlocutor, who is more than likely fascinated by the figure of the current Pontiff. Pope Francis calls insistently — for example, in the Apostolic Exhortation *Evangelii Gaudium* — for a missionary effort to re-evangelize those of the baptized for whom the faith has become irrelevant, and also to evangelize those who have not yet received an explicit announcement of the Good News. From this point of view, the Tridentine Mass offers abundant resources. Its well-known characteristics of sacrality, orientation *ad Deum*, the affirmation of the creaturely condition before the Creator and Redeemer, the use of a complete symbolic and synesthetic language (the Tridentine liturgy involves all the internal and external senses of man), and the concentration of the message, all constitute a sort of fundamental announcement of the Gospel that strikes the one who perceives it in a theologically and anthropologically potent way.

The legend about the conversion of the Russian prince Vladimir to Christianity that marks the entrance of the Russian people into the Christian family is significant here. The prince sent his emissaries into the surrounding lands to seek information about the true religion. When they returned, they related how in Constantinople, in the Basilica of Hagia Sophia, they had assisted at the splendid Eastern liturgy and had drawn this conclusion: "We did not know whether we were on earth or already in heaven." Yes, dear friends, there is a great need to evangelize the world, and the liturgy celebrated fittingly is a potent instrument because it is God Himself who acts through it in the world. Permit me to cite the text of the 35th proposition of the 2012 Synod of Bishops dedicated to evangelization, and too soon forgotten in the vicious media bombardment of the next synod:[3]

> The worthy celebration of the sacred liturgy, God's most treasured gift to us, is the source of the highest expression of our life in Christ (cf. *Sacrosanctum Concilium*, 10). It is, therefore, the primary and most powerful expression of the new evangelization. God desires to manifest the incomparable beauty of his immeasurable and unceasing love for us through the sacred liturgy, and we, for our part, desire to employ what is most beautiful in our worship of God in response to his gift. In the marvelous exchange of the sacred liturgy, by which heaven descends to earth, salvation is at hand, calling forth repentance and conversion of heart (cf. Mt 4:17; Mk 1:15). Evangelization in the Church calls

---

3 That is, the Extraordinary General Synod, "The Pastoral Challenges of the Family in the Context of Evangelization," held in 2014.

for a liturgy that lifts the hearts of men and women to God. The liturgy is not just a human action but an encounter with God which leads to contemplation and deepening friendship with God. In this sense, the liturgy of the Church is the best school of the faith.[4]

Given this definition of liturgy, and seeing its intrinsic role, insofar as it is a divine action, in the success of evangelization and the consolidation of the faith, one cannot help but associate these words with the rites of the Tridentine Mass, venerable in their sobriety, solemn in their simplicity, and divine in their beauty. Yes, dear friends, let us affirm it with joy and conviction: we would have a great surge of evangelization and mission work, exactly the sort Pope Francis has asked for, if we had a wider diffusion of the Tridentine Mass.

A MASS FOR THE GOOD OF SOULS

The second reason is also inspired by the current pontificate. It is appropriate, one might say, that a theologian pope has been succeeded by a pastoral pope who orients even theology toward the pastoral. What does "pastoral" mean, exactly? It means to take care of souls, or persons to use more modern language. It is biblically symbolized in the figure of the sheep. The care of souls — I like to use this phrase because everyone understands it well — does it not mean to communicate the greatest good, which is divine grace? And what is the source of divine grace if not the Sacrifice of the Cross that is mystically renewed in the celebration of the Mass? And because the mystical reality

4   The text may be found at http://www.vatican.va/news_services/press/sinodo/documents/bollettino_25_xiii-ordinaria-2012/02_inglese/b33_02.html.

of the unbloody sacrifice is expressed through a language of signs — which is to say, a sacramental language — the more it is comprehensible, the more the soul will be disposed to receiving the goods of divine grace. The liturgical language of the Tridentine Mass — some may be surprised to hear it — is more comprehensible to me. Naturally, one must first define the content to be comprehended. We have just said it: it is divine grace, that is, a spiritual good different from what we experience in daily human life, a spiritual good that surprises, as Holy Mary "full of grace" was surprised at the Angel's annunciation, a spiritual good that requires of us a willing acceptance full of wonder, adoration, gratitude, and silence; in short, the attitudes the believer cultivates in the type of *participatio actuosa* facilitated by the Tridentine Mass. Essentially, the good of souls demands a Mass founded in grace, in which grace is perceived in all the "otherness" proper to it insofar as it is a divine gift.

On this note, I recall reading an article some time ago on a Spanish-language blog. The crux of the argument was that laymen who participate regularly in the Tridentine Mass are challenged to live the obligations of the Christian life to the full extent that common human frailty allows: from fidelity to the obligations they assume in the sacrament of matrimony, to honesty and consistency in the exercise of their professions. It is far from our intent to invent classifications of A- and B-level Christians. Thanks be to God, it is the Eternal Father who establishes these rankings, and He does so with immense mercy, as Pope Francis rightly insists. Nevertheless, it is an objective fact that the lay faithful who love the Tridentine Mass find, in a most evident way, abundant spiritual resources for being faithful spouses, fertile parents, responsible educators, honest citizens, obedient believers, charitable neighbors, and penitents who confess frequently. In the times we live in, this blessing is both precious and rare! My experience has been that the faithful I know who love the Tridentine Mass usually belong to this category. Thus a question has come to my mind: given the gallimaufry of pastoral projects, plans of intervention, itineraries and journeys of various sorts, emanating from an often garrulous ecclesiastical bureaucracy, which seem to produce few effects, is it not opportune to propose an initiation into the traditional liturgy? *Videant consules.*[5]

AN EXCELLENT SCHOOL OF PRIESTLY PIETY

Now I will speak of my own class: priests. I think that their situation is generally good when compared with other ages in the history of the Church. At least this is true from a qualitative point of view, since vast regions are suffering from a lack of priests and Masses. The formative foundation is sound: a seminary, a *ratio studiorum*, formators, and advisers. Certainly, situations vary from region to region, sometimes diocese to diocese. One of the weak points in the average priest is a weak cultural formation caused by any number of factors. Further, even at the end of the formative course, he often has a spotty, superficial, and badly ordered theological formation. Let me explain: it is spotty because some subjects are not studied, like apologetics (and the results are apparent: the world insults Christianity to the face and priests do not know how to respond) or angelology (and many priests do not know how to do an exorcism — assuming they even believe in the existence of the devil, who is wreaking havoc today, despite Pope Francis's

5 A reference to the ancient Roman decree: *videant consules ne quid res publica detrimenti capiat*, let the Consuls see to it that no harm befall the State.

frequent warnings). It is superficial because they are unable to approach the sources of theology in Latin and Greek and must rely on the cultural mediations of translations and summaries. It is disordered because they study a great many subjects, courses, and lessons, but lack a Christocentric-Trinitarian foundation, which must be that of the *Catechism of the Catholic Church*, including creed, liturgy, morality, and spiritual life.

Now if a priest becomes familiar with the older Roman Missal, every day he makes an excellent review of theology. With access to that source of all sources, he finds everything essential presented in an ordered schema. In the Missal of 1962, the priest finds a great amount of the Bible, especially in the Psalms that form the foundation of the antiphons. He finds the Fathers' Scripture commentaries in the euchological patrimony. He runs through the mysteries of salvation history. He is immersed in the expressions which have carried the content of the faith throughout the centuries, expressions in which the great dogmas concerning creation, sin, redemption, sanctification, and eternal life have been formulated. And note well, it is not a verbose theology, a bit arrogant, frequently tedious, as often appears in the classrooms of a theology faculty, but a theology that is, as it were, silent like the Roman Canon, humble because the priest performs it on his knees, wonderful because he sees it with the Body of Christ between his hands.

For these reasons, the Tridentine Mass is an excellent school of priestly piety. I stress just one point here. Priests are always busy. They enter the sacristy in haste, put on their vestments in haste (perhaps this is one of the reasons they were reduced to the bare essential), in haste he ascends the altar. The Tridentine Mass ensures that the priest recites beautiful prayers as he vests, before leaving the sacristy and when standing before the altar.

He enters a dimension of time where there is no more reason to move hastily. The light of eternity enwraps him. I urge all my brother priests: get to know the Tridentine Mass. Its theology and spirituality burn hot with the Holy Spirit!

AN EFFICACIOUS WEAPON AGAINST THE DEVIL

Should we be pessimists or reasonable optimists about how things are going in the world? To tell the truth, whenever we begin to make a list of things that are not going well, we always fear being denounced as "prophets of doom." But I will not venture upon these considerations because, for one thing, I would not like to sin against the second theological virtue, and for another because one would need to be a specialist in every field in order to understand how things are going. There are not many omniscient people these days, but I gladly leave the task to them.

Yet of one thing, dear friends, I am certain. The devil and his minions have been granted a great share of liberty in recent times. This conviction comes from my conversations with exorcists, who have a great deal to say to us today. Is there not a Luciferian spirit in the current fashion of denying the harmony of creation found in sexual difference, to except oneself from this order and cry more shrilly each day, even into the faces of innocent children: "*Non obœdiam*"? Is it not a Satanic hatred which now causes, according to well-attested statistics, the violent death of one Christian every day, and has introduced the word *Christianophobia* into modern parlance? Truly the devil is working, and when he works, he has a preferred victim: the Church. Mad with rage, unable to do anything against the Bridegroom, he turns to His Spouse. We must defend ourselves, or else we'll take every hit and be the worse for it.

Like it or not, the Tridentine Mass has a sacramental language objectively more complete and efficacious for opposing the action of the devil. It suffers none of the rationalistic hesitations of another Missal against calling the evil one by name and begging God the Father to help us in the fight. Rather, to press the point, just as the priest who offers the sacrifice acts *in persona Christi*, so it is Jesus Christ Himself, Our Lord, who prays the Father to sustain the Church against the devil. What can we do alone? Should we deploy rifles against missiles? Rather, we enter combat in the ranks of the General, Jesus Christ, and turn the battle over to Him. And we are never alone: there are the saints and angels of heaven, including the Archangel Michael whom Pope Leo XIII ordered to be invoked at the end of every Mass. Is it unreasonable to think that if we recover this practice through the *Vetus Ordo* and take it up again in the *Novus Ordo*, things might go a little better?

A WAY OF BEAUTY POINTING TO HEAVEN

The Tridentine Mass is beautiful, and the *via pulchritudinis* is an excellent *itinerarium in Deum*.[6]

Its language, Latin, the sacred language *par excellence*, is beautiful.

The disposition of the altar is beautiful, with the crucifix in a central position instead of the priest who, as charming as he may be, cannot be compared to the crucifix.

The atmosphere of recollection is beautiful; the music is beautiful.

The humility of the faithful is beautiful, on their knees before the communion rail; beautiful, too, the faith that shines through the eyes of the old, who know how to adore the One

6 "way of beauty ... path to God."

who has accompanied them in the various stages of their lives, who descends to the altar for this very reason, and who will gather them into heaven.

Beautiful is the innocence of the children, who are sometimes discontented, but who will never fail to observe that if Mom and Dad are kneeling, He before whom they kneel must be more important than Mom and Dad.

The piety of the young is beautiful, when at the beginning of the rite they repeat those immortal words, "ad Deum qui laetificat iuventutem meam."[7]

The testimony of the priest is beautiful, who in his ministry is doing everything he can to do the people good, but if he fails, at the end of Mass when he recites the *Placeat* he knows that he has done the most important thing for them.

The company of the saints of Paradise, whose names are frequently invoked and whose intercession is frequently implored, especially that of Holy Mary, is also beautiful.

And She is beautiful, the Queen of Heaven, who stood with John the Apostle on Calvary and stands near us now in every unbloody renewal of the Sacrifice of the Cross, as only the Tridentine Mass knows how to show us.

To Her I entrust the desires we cherish in our hearts that the Tridentine Mass will spread, restored so generously to the Church by a great pope, Benedictus Magnus, "ad laudem et gloriam nominis sui, ad utilitatem quoque nostram totiusque ecclesiae suae sanctae."[8]

---

7 "to God, who giveth joy to my youth" (Ps 42:4), from the prayers at the foot of the altar.

8 "to the praise and glory of His Name, to our own benefit, and to that of all His Holy Church": from the response to the *Orate, fratres* at the end of the Offertory.

−2−

The *Vetus Ordo Missae* for a "Church Going Forth"†

Honored ladies, distinguished gentlemen, dear friends,

I AM HONORED TO HAVE RECEIVED AN invitation to this gathering. Our meeting is held in Lecce—one of the capitals of art and culture in southern Italy, and the seat of a vivacious coetus *Summorum Pontificum*, where the national coordinator Dr. Capoccia is based. We owe the splendid pilgrimage days of October 2014—in the presence of the *grandi cardinali* so esteemed by the great Pope Emeritus—to his initiative. This kind of gathering helps us to reflect on the spiritual riches of the *Vetus Ordo Missae*, that authentic thesaurus of doctrine and piety that Benedict XVI has restored to the Church intact, so that it may continue to accomplish its mission in history: to give glory to God and to be an instrument of grace for the salvation of souls.

A CHALLENGE

The reflections I intend to share are based on a concern of which, I am sure, none of us is unaware. It is an objection on the part of those who look with little sympathy on the *Vetus Ordo*, a challenge we could formulate in this way: the extraordinary form of the Roman liturgy is an anachronism, divorced from the Church's current life and needs as indicated by the

† A LECTURE GIVEN IN LECCE, MARCH 2015.

pontificate of Francis, who is urging the Church to make a bold pastoral turn toward the peripheries of the world, without hesitation or retreat. The world's poverty calls for options very different from that of an ancient ritualism that is incomprehensible to modern sensibilities. Some go even further in their evaluation of the Tridentine liturgy, saying that there is an insurmountable distance between the magisterium of the current pope and the groups who promote the Mass in Latin. In order to *sentire cum ecclesia*,[1] it is necessary, therefore, to renounce the *liturgia antiquior*.

I see the matter differently. I maintain, in fact, that the Tridentine Mass offers a resource for realizing the program that the Supreme Pontiff has espoused in the most relevant and authoritative document of his magisterium to date, the Apostolic Exhortation *Evangelii Gaudium*, summed up in the already well-known expression "a Church that goes forth."

What he means by "a Church that goes forth" is illustrated in n. 24: "The Church which 'goes forth' is a community of missionary disciples who take the first step, who are involved and supportive, who bear fruit and rejoice."[2] We should read this citation alongside another, drawn from the passage immediately preceding. Here Francis explains that the actions of these disciples, which constitute the movement of the Church going forth, is nothing other than what we call evangelization and mission. We have to take the initiative, involve ourselves, accompany, bear fruit, and rejoice because there is a content to transmit — the Gospel, the good news!

1 "think with the Church," be of the same mind or judgment as the Church.

2 Francis, Apostolic Exhortation *Evangelii Gaudium* (November 24, 2013), n. 24.

Evangelization obeys the missionary mandate of Jesus: "Go therefore and make disciples of all nations, baptizing them in the name of the Father and of the Son and of the Holy Spirit, and teaching them to obey everything that I have commanded you." Today in this "Go" of Jesus are present all the scenarios and challenges of the evangelical mission of the Church, and we are all called to this new missionary "going forth."[3]

A Church that "goes forth" means, therefore, nothing more or less than a missionary Church that evangelizes people and their cultures, a task that must be undertaken in the diverse situations and numerous challenges of the world today.

The Latin Mass is certainly part of this ecclesiology of "going forth," and this for three sets of reasons: doctrinal, spiritual, and pastoral.

DOCTRINAL REASONS

Before testifying, before accompanying, before celebrating, the community of disciples who "go forth" and reach the existential peripheries do not arrive empty-handed. They pass on their most precious treasure to the men and women they encounter, their own reason for existence: their faith in our Lord Jesus Christ. The Supreme Pontiff has reminded us of this, citing the words of the missionary mandate that is valid for all times: "Teach and observe all that I have commanded you."

My dear friends, my claim is that the *Vetus Ordo* is a *summarium*, a summary of the teachings and commandments of Our Lord. "What are the two principal mysteries of the faith?" asked

3   Ibid., n. 19.

the timeless catechism of St Pius X. "The unity and Trinity of God; the Incarnation, Passion, and death of Jesus Christ."

Using a ritual language composed of gestures and speech, the *Vetus Ordo Missae* is a dialogue going out from the Holy Trinity and returning to the Most Holy Trinity. Take one example. In the priestly prayers, the priest twice addresses himself directly to the Holy Trinity: first, at the conclusion of the Offertory when he implores the three Divine Persons to receive the offering presented in memory of the Passion and glorification of Jesus Christ and in honor of His Mother and the saints: "Suscipe, Sancta Trinitas, hanc oblationem . . ." At the end of Mass, the priest begs the Holy Trinity to accept the offering that the Son has renewed. And how could the Three Divine Persons refuse the propitiatory gift of Jesus Christ: "Placeat tibi, Sancta Trinitas, hoc obsequium servitutis meae . . ."? Unfortunately, these two prayers have disappeared in the *Novus Ordo Missae*, and what's more, in the Ordinary of the Mass, the Most Holy Trinity is never expressly mentioned, not even once. This is rather curious, to say the least.

The second principal mystery of the faith, the Incarnation, is constantly recalled in the celebration of the extraordinary form. What do the faithful who assist at this Mass see? Physically, they see a crucifix depicting the second Person of the Holy Trinity, the one who became Incarnate and suffered for our salvation. In this way, the *lex credendi* penetrates with luminous simplicity into the *lex orandi*. The *Vetus Ordo* presents, in all their integrity and essential nature, the divine teachings that together form the content of the evangelical mission of the Church "going forth."

We could multiply examples to show how the Tridentine Mass, *in se et per se*, is a sort of catechism for everyone, suited for evangelizing both believers and non-believers alike. We see, for instance, that the framework of salvation history — creation, sin, Incarnation, redemption, grace, glory, and eternal life — is assumed into the prayers in words that recall the teaching, not of a postconciliar liturgical expert (however great), but of the Fathers of the Church, men of the stature of a St Leo the Great. For example, there are the words the priest pronounces at the moment of the pouring of water into the chalice:

> Deus qui humanae substantiae dignitatem mirabiliter condidisti [*creation*] et mirabilius reformasti [*redemption*], da nobis per huius aquae et vini mysterium eius divinitatis esse consortes [*divinization or the life of grace*], qui humanitatis nostrae fieri dignatus est particeps [*Incarnation*].[4]

Again, is not the drama of sin physically embodied and existentially invoked in the gestures of the *Confiteor*, when we kneel, beat our chests, and repeat the words and hearken to the absolution of the priest? This prayer — "Indulgentiam, absolutionem, et remissionem peccatorum vestrorum tribuat vobis omnipotens et misericors Dominus"[5] — was unfortunately abolished in the *Novus Ordo*. Yet it seems like an echo of the words of the Holy Father Pope Francis, who has repeatedly told us that God is good, indulgent, merciful!

Further, in the Roman Canon, the priest asks the Father

---

4 "O God, who didst wonderfully establish the dignity of human nature, and still more wonderfully didst restore it: grant us, through the mystery of this water and wine, that we may be made sharers of His divinity, who deigned to become a partaker in our humanity."

5 "May the almighty and merciful Lord grant you pardon, absolution, and remission of your sins."

that we and those whom we meet in our journeys "going forth" may arrive after such a long way at the end of the road, and all go forth from this world to pass the final judgment, the only judgment about which we need to concern ourselves, even though we do it serenely because the Madonna, whose intercession is often recalled in the old Mass, prays for us: "ab aeterna damnatione nos eripi et in electorum tuorum iubeas grege numerari."[6] "Go out, brethren," the pope asks us, "evangelize," "teach" what the Divine Teacher has communicated to us. And while, in filial attachment and obedience to the Holy Father, we close the doors of our churches to go out and hurry toward the nations, the peoples, the cultures we have to evangelize, we will carry with us the Missal — the one the faithful page through in bilingual and pocket editions when assisting at the Holy Mass, and which, therefore, they know almost by memory: it is our preferred catechism.

I'd like briefly to add another consideration. Even as the *Novus Ordo* has introduced the sacrosanct principle that the rite should be adapted to the pastoral needs of the community, it has involuntarily left itself open to a blow that has landed with a series of unfortunate consequences: it has permitted the priest and others with liturgical roles — heedless of the distinction between what can be modified and what should never be modified — to introduce elements entirely extraneous to the *lex credendi*. In the name of liturgical creativity (not the same as adaptation), doctrinal errors can be taught inadvertently, even very grave ones. The extraordinary form, for its part, guards the purity of Christian doctrine in an indestructible chest of

6   "Snatch us from eternal damnation and command that we be numbered among the flock of Thine elect."

sacrality. How can we deprive men and women, who have the right to receive the authentic Christian faith, of the riches of the treasures of knowledge and divine wisdom? In this way, do we not betray the missionary mandate, when in the place of the faith of the Church, we recklessly proclaim our own personal opinions?

SPIRITUAL REASONS

The second reason, of a spiritual nature, applies to those who carry out evangelization, those who — to remain faithful to the image employed by Pope Francis — "go forth." He himself has spoken about "situations" and "challenges" that oppose the Gospel. Sometimes he has called them by name, and with just severity. Let's recall them here with rapid brush strokes.

On one hand, there is anthropological and moral relativism that does not admit any objective truth. It tends to manifest itself in that sort of right to free thinking denounced by Pope Benedict in the memorable *Missa pro eligendo Romano Pontifice* of 2005. The faithful who go forth and encounter this situation, so prevalent in the weary and desperate Western world, encounter indifference, marginalization, and derision. The nihilism that grips contemporary networks of communication and the decision centers of the world of finance and politics, often imposes a sort of white martyrdom. This is what we are all exposed to. On the peripheries, or the Eastern part of the world, especially where the radical form of Islam holds sway, the believers "going forth," and even those who prudently remain at home, undergo a bloody or semi-bloody martyrdom caused by vexations of various kinds. According to trustworthy statistics, the numbers are horrifying: every five minutes a Christian is killed. As of this year, a new word has been added to the dictionary, one with a sinister sense: Christianophobia. The Church "going forth" of the twenty-first century is a Church of martyrdom.

It is unfortunate that shepherds with grave responsibilities and Catholic intellectuals who have wide audiences, even those who style themselves the curators of what they call, in a rather dubious expression, the "Church of Francis," forget this drama that ought to have an absolute priority in the teaching and action of the Church "going forth." It is true that the *Vetus Ordo Missae* is not the "happening" party to which, often, we painfully see the Sacrifice of Christ on the altar reduced. It is the Mass in which we all climb mystically to the mount of Calvary, and not just for a pleasant morning stroll. We are immersed in a story of persecution, that of the Holy Innocent *par excellence*; His blood is poured out, His Passion is renewed; the Martyr at the head of all the martyrs is immolated on the altar. Here the believer is escorted, admonished, prepared to confront his martyrdom, whether it is white or bloody.

The *Vetus Ordo Missae* is a school of evangelization. It is so not because it offers courses in theology for the laity, taught (if only!) by serious professors in clerical suits ready to present the theologoumena of some exponent of theology *à la page*. It is a school of evangelization because it disposes missionaries "going forth" to confront and measure themselves against the world, which — ever since St John the Evangelist wrote his Prologue, proclaimed in almost every Tridentine Mass — refuses the light, remains in the shadows of error and violence, and fights the Gospel, not metaphorically but with bloody seriousness. The Church "going forth" is a Church militant, as it was once called, and even if it is not called that anymore, it always will be so, as our brethren persecuted for the faith know only too well.

PASTORAL REASONS

According to *Evangelii Gaudium*, the Church "going forth"
works for a "pastoral conversion."[7] Like all the pithy expressions of Pope Francis, this one merits further explanation. I
think we can give an authentic interpretation to the thought
and intentions of the Holy Father if by "pastoral" conversion
we mean the assumption of a perspective of ecclesial action
that takes its point of departure from and measures itself constantly according to the psychological, moral, and spiritual
needs of the people, buffeted as they are by the sorrows of life,
of contemporary life in particular. This is nothing more than
the solicitude of the Good Shepherd, who moved among the
crowd because the people were like "sheep without a shepherd"
(Mk 6:34). To keep within the ambit of the Gospel image, it
is interesting to note what Christ the Good Shepherd decides
to do, with regard to the smell of those sheep abandoned and
stricken. The same Evangelist relates that "He began to teach
them many things." That is, He offers them healthy and nour-
ishing food; not emotions or experiences, but good doctrine,
because the Good Shepherd is the Good Teacher and the Good
Teacher is the Good Shepherd, the same one who teaches the
indissolubility of marriage. Those who oppose doctrine and
pastoral practice in their pastoral and disciplinary choices do
not act according to the method of the Good Shepherd.

Fine then: what does all this have to do with the old Mass?
So much! In order to encounter the exigencies of the suffering,
what can pastors today offer to their flocks? Their sympathy,
their piety, their patient attention, their solidarity? Certainly
this, but this is very little. Pastors can and must offer divine

7 See *Evangelii Gaudium*, nn. 27, 32.

grace. What a marvelous reality! The Gospel speaks about it for the first time in the sweetest scene it has transmitted to us: the Annunciation to Holy Mary, full of grace. Wherever there is grace, at Nazareth or in any other place in history where human liberty opens itself to God, behold, the divine Word operates in the power of the Holy Spirit, with the cooperation of the Mother of God, and life, light, consolation, peace, purity, sanctity, gifts and perfections, virtues and fruits inundate the human soul. Divine grace is offered to us principally and ordinarily through the sacramental economy, of which the Holy Mass is the source and summit, fulcrum and motor, because there the Eucharistic Heart of Our Lord continues to pour out His treasures, "blood and water," as John the Evangelist observes (Jn 19:34).

Of course I don't intend to affirm that the *Vetus Ordo Missae* has an exclusive claim on grace and that the ordinary form is not an abundant dispenser of it. Absolutely not. However, the Tridentine Mass generates a liturgical-spiritual culture that exalts the action of grace. Indeed, while the Mass in the ordinary form gives emphasis to the exterior participation of the faithful and the minister, it interprets *participatio actuosa* (active participation) in terms of a plurality of gestures, and thus expresses in its ritual a certain human agency. In the old Mass, each word and each silence, each gesture and each rite is broadened and elevated to create a truly supernatural tension that can open up a human space, enlarging the soul and its faculties — like the most pure womb of the Virgin Mary and her Immaculate Heart — to gather grace. God is the protagonist and the only actor, and grace is poured out copiously in order to be humbly received, gathered, guarded, fructified. "Bear fruit": this is the phrase used by Pope Francis to describe what the Church "going forth" should do. Grace cleanses, grace heals, grace renews: this is the medicine administered in the field hospital.

Dear friends, the current pontificate seems to stir up enthusiasm in a large part of the faithful. Are our pastors at various levels, besides citing the expressions used by Francis (which undoubtedly have a notable communicative efficacy), really and seriously translating this invitation to evangelization and to mission into concrete actions, so that — as *Evangelii Gaudium* 24 reminds us — men and women of our time, in their various circumstances of history and geography, receive the teachings and commandments of Our Lord? I am certainly not in a place to respond to this question. However, especially where resources are very scarce, I would venture to ask our pastors to investigate the doctrinal, spiritual, and pastoral riches of the *Vetus Ordo Missae* and that *forma fidei et caritatis*[8] which tradition — of which the Tridentine Mass is the most precious jewel — offers the Church "going forth" today and yesterday, ever since the divine Word was sent from Heaven to live in the immaculate womb of Mary and the Holy Spirit blew into the hearts of the Apostles at Pentecost — so that she may be a sign and instrument of salvation. This Mass was the Mass of the zealous missionaries, intrepid confessors, venerable pastors, courageous martyrs, in short of a Church authentically "going forth."

Nec plura. Dixi. Gratias.[9]

8 "form (expression, model) of faith and charity"
9 "That is all. I have spoken. Thank you."

Desperate Times Call for
Desperate Measures

THE URGENCY OF SPREADING
THE MASS OF THE OLD RITE[†]

Honored ladies, distinguished gentlemen, dear friends,

I AM PLEASED AND HONORED TO BE able to speak to all of you this evening. You represent a significant vanguard of faithful who promote the celebration of the Holy Mass in the extraordinary form of the Roman rite with zeal and competence. We find ourselves in Naples, ancient and glorious capital of the splendid Kingdom of Italy before the unification, the homeland of Saint Alphonsus Liguori and of so many other saints who have loved the Holy Sacrifice of the Mass and the Most Holy Sacrament of the Eucharist. They have transmitted an inheritance of faith and religious culture that you worthily receive through your generous activities for the spread of the Tridentine Mass. This apostolic effort has in our days taken on a character of extreme urgency, because the dangers and challenges facing the Church and society are extreme. Hence the title, perhaps a bit journalistic, of the reflection I intend to present today. My thoughts can be divided into three points: first, the Mass of the *Vetus Ordo* reasserts the order of reality; second, its special qualities

† A LECTURE GIVEN IN NAPLES, APRIL 2015.

powerfully oppose the work of Satan; third, the spreading of this form of Mass is an outstanding spiritual work of mercy.

THE MASS OF THE *VETUS ORDO* REASSERTS THE ORDER OF THINGS

I begin from a fact apparent to everyone: our society, especially but not exclusively in Western countries, has passed through a period of devastating disintegration, and the life of people everywhere has been immersed in a climate of moral corruption that makes the conscience sick. The aggressions perpetrated by the gay lobby to impose gender theory, defined by the current Supreme Pontiff on the occasion of his pastoral visit right here in Naples as an "erroneous mentality," "foolishness," is the most acute and emblematic expression of this anthropological disaster, resonating in the opinions diffused by the communications media, imposed by parliamentary assemblies, and setting its roots in ever more widespread habits of behavior.[1] The collapse of the institution of the family, desired and accomplished with Satanic tenacity by articles of legislation, has caused significant repercussions in these countries' economies; it has induced emotional immaturity and existential confusion not only in the young but now even in adults deprived in their infancy of their right to live in anything resembling a family, and who frequently opt for unstable or unnatural cohabitation; it has injected a lethal virus into the families, the cells of the Church herself, placing many believers in irregular situations and even inducing some pastors to hypothesize pastoral projects whose audacity leaves us utterly dismayed.

1 Francis, "Incontro con i giovani a Napoli," March 21, 2015, http://w2.vatican.va/content/francesco/it/speeches/2015/march/documents/papa-francesco_20150321_napoli-pompei-giovani.html.

The crisis of contemporary society can be discerned empirically in the phenomena I have just mentioned, though they represent only an exemplary and certainly not an exhaustive sample of the whole. They are part of an historical-cultural process that is more vast and profound. This process has been documented, among others, by a school of thought largely constituted by advocates from Catholic backgrounds, known as "counter-revolutionary." In the last century, the major representative of this vision of history was the Brazilian intellectual Plinio Corrêa de Oliveira, author of a profound essay, presented in theses rather than argumentation, entitled "Revolution and Counter-Revolution."[2] Giovanni Cantoni, perhaps the best Italian interpreter of the counter-revolutionary thought of Plinio Corrêa de Oliveira, synthesizes its central idea:

> There once existed a Western civilization that was Christian, animated by the Catholic Church, fruit of the faith's enculturation in the West. We are now witnessing the process of this Christian civilization's destruction, the Revolution, a historical dynamic in four phases. The first phase was religious, the Protestant Reformation, preceded and accompanied by a cultural revolution represented by Humanism and the Renaissance. The second was political, the French Revolution; the third social, the Communist Revolution; and last, the fourth, the cultural revolution initiated in France in '68.[3]

2   A PDF version is available at www.tfp.org/revolution-and-counter-revolution/.

3   Cf. G. Cantoni's introduction to the essay of Plinio Corrêa de Oliveira, *Rivoluzione e contro-rivoluzione*, from Sugarco Publications.

This process has ruptured the order founded by God in creation, restored and perfected in the work of redemption. In the Protestant Reformation, the balance in Christian faith between Scripture and Tradition, and the balance in the Church between charism and authority, was altered. After dealing a heavy blow to the unity of Christianity, the Revolution advanced in the Enlightenment and the French Revolution, when reason withdrew from its friendship with faith and, proudly declaring its self-sufficiency, produced monsters of ideological and political totalitarianism, which dramatically and violently erupted into European and world history in the following century. In the next phase, the Marxist-Leninist, the Revolution subverted the social order, driven by the illusion of an unnatural egalitarianism that, wherever it is asserted with force, has caused moral and material misery, sadness and tedium, intolerance and violence.

We are in the fourth phase of the Revolution: no longer only the religious order, or the cultural, or even the social, but the natural order is being uprooted by the Revolution. The fundamental structure of man is denied when heterosexual marriage is abolished and what is inscribed in human nature is declared a fruit of personal decision or sexual identity. We are in the final phase of the encounter between two opposed and irreducible anthropologies: the one God has given to us in creation and the one the devil spreads abroad, aping the Creator by his crafty, malignant destructive action mendaciously presented as an affirmation of human liberty over nature herself. The monstrosities of genetic engineering and of certain assisted conception practices enter into this fearsome struggle. The Revolution can be summarized in these terms: man puts himself in the place of God, in a foolish act of *hubris*, always freighted with dire consequences.

Dear friends, what does any of this have to do with the Mass of the old rite? And especially, what can we do, humble successors of David, numerically few, with our meek and peaceful Tridentine rites, when faced with the apparently invincible power of Goliath, who marches pompously and seemingly triumphantly through the centuries and lands of the world? There is most definitely a connection! We, who are spreading the ancient Mass with our apostolic action, are collecting (even without realizing it) our five spiritual stones to sling against the great villain. It is a historical fact not to be undervalued that, when the Revolution began with the Protestant Reformation, the Counter-Revolution opposed it through the inspired decisions of the Fathers of the Council of Trent, defining the Mass as a sacrifice and professing our faith in the real Eucharistic presence. The council was followed by the publication in 1570 of the *Missale Romanum* of St Pius V — the Missal that, with certain adjustments and additions, was last promulgated in a new edition in 1962 by St John XXIII. In our time, Pope Benedict has restored the use of it to the entire Church.

But what I would like to say is that, *in se* and *per se*, the ancient Mass — let us call it that in order to indicate its chronological place in a pre- and therefore also post-revolutionary epic — is instrumental in arresting the revolutionary process and stimulating the counter-revolution toward the recovery of a civilization at once human and Christian. It reasserts the order denied by the Revolution. The ritual of the *usus antiquior*, in fact, expresses so well — I might say perfectly, without any gaps or defects — the relation between man and God. The presence of God and the good He does to save us are placed in clear evidence: in the center we find the crucifix, the altar, the tabernacle, rather than liturgical signs referring to man, such as the priest who presides, a banquet table, the gathered assembly. In other words, the old rite Mass is theocentric and not anthropocentric. Before God the Creator and Redeemer, the old rite invites us to assume the only possible and reasonable attitude: humility.

Humility is more than a virtue. It is the condition for a virtuous life. Watch the bows and genuflections the humble man makes faithfully before God in a spirit of obedience, acknowledging His merciful sovereignty, His love without bounds, His creative wisdom. Reason is not tempted to be puffed up, as happens in the revolutionary process, because in the old rite not everything can or ought to be explained by reason which, for its part, is content to adore God without comprehending Him. It turns to Him through the means of a sacred language differing from ordinary speech, because in the harmonious order of creation that the liturgy represents in its rituals, there is never a monotonous repetition or tedious uniformity, but a symphony of diversity, sacred and profane, without opposition, respecting the alterity of each. Here reason also renounces an excessive use of words that unfortunately exists in the liturgical praxis inaugurated by the *Novus Ordo*, interpreted by many priests as the opportunity for pure garrulousness. In the old rite, on the other hand, reason appeals to other dimensions of communication and, besides words pronounced or sung, also gives silence a place. This silence becomes the atmosphere, impregnated with the Holy Spirit, in which believing thought and prayerful word is born.

The absurd pretense of the Revolution to eliminate the differences that make up the *ordines sociales*[4] can also intrude itself in

---

4 "social orders"; the various natural and supernatural orders by which a society is constituted.

the form of an ecclesiology that denies the distinction between the baptismal and ministerial priesthood. There is absolutely none of this in the old rite, which attributes a precise role to every actor of the divine liturgy, with an emphasis upon the action of the priest who represents Christ, the Mediator and Recapitulator in whom every creature finds its place in the order of the cosmos redeemed by Him. See, if we delve into the treasures of the extraordinary form of the Roman rite, as Pope Benedict has defined it, we draw out something *vetera et nova* (old and new) and give a push to the counter-revolutionary work of restoring the order of things willed by God and denied by the devil. This work is urgent: we cannot tarry any longer.

AGAINST THE WORK OF SATAN

Besides the revolutionary process, there is today, as always, the extreme evil of Satan's work. St Paul declares it without mincing words: "For our struggle is not against enemies of flesh and blood, but against the rulers, against the authorities, against the cosmic powers of this present darkness, against the spiritual forces of evil in the heavenly places" (Eph 6:12).

It might seem that today, perhaps more than in the past, the devil and his underlings have been granted greater liberty of action. Not only do they challenge the created order, as we said before, and in their rebellion shout their "Non serviam" (I will not serve); they conduct an implacable war against the Church, the most beautiful and fertile fruit of the redemption: the persecutions of yesterday and today are not unrelated to the devil's hatred. We have noted the vision of Pope Leo XIII, after which he wrote the prayer to St Michael the Archangel to be recited after Mass, a vision in which he perceived a storm of aggression of infernal beings against the

Church. It seems that the devil has orchestrated his wicked designs not only from the outside, but even from the inside. From this point of view we can understand the fears of Pope Paul VI. In a memorable discourse held in 1972, he spoke of "the smoke of Satan entering the Church through some crack."[5] Recent phenomena in the life of the Church would appear to confirm that this pestilential smoke is diffusing itself not only through cracks, as Pope Montini, who was a cultured and authentically modern Pontiff, warned, but through clefts and openings much more gaping.

What are we to do? We fight the devil with what he fears the most, using the weapons he cannot defeat. For one, we take the Rosary in hand, just as so many souls have done during the ancient Mass, even if our super-liturgists and super-pastoralists, who have never assisted at an exorcism where the Rosary beads are an object of loathing to the possessed, refer to these faithful souls with pompous sneers or grimaces of disgust. Further, we adore Our Lord in the Holy Eucharist, under the appearances of bread and wine. An exorcist once said: "I would have all priests take part in an exorcism. Their way of celebrating Mass would change, because the devil, in his own way, has faith in the Real Presence and knows well what transubstantiation is." Yes, the devil is put to flight by the Church through the celebration of the Holy Mass because in every Mass, the Body and Blood, Soul and Divinity of Our Lord Jesus Christ, with all their salvific efficacy, are given to believers to fight the good fight against Satan and his allies.

5   Paul VI, Homily for the Solemnity of the Holy Apostles Peter and Paul, June 29, 1972, a summary of which may be found at http://w2.vatican.va/content/paul-vi/it/homilies/1972/documents/hf_p-vi_hom_19720629.html.

Objectively speaking, the old rite of Mass expresses faith in the Real Presence with greater devotion and, I would dare to say, conviction, than the *Novus Ordo*. We all know well enough the ritual gestures of prostration before the Eucharist, as the *lex credendi* becomes the *lex orandi*. Every time the hands of the priests must enter into contact with the consecrated species, he genuflects, much more frequently in the *Vetus Ordo* than in the *Novus Ordo*. Vigilant and diligent care is taken so that not even a fragment of the consecrated Host may be lost: think of the joining of the thumb and index finger by the priest from the moment of the consecration until the final ablutions, or of the use of the corporal and the other sacred linens. At the moment of the consecration, all the gazes of the faithful are joined, as rivers into an ocean of love, in adoration of the consecrated species. It is moving and edifying to see the faithful of every age and condition kneel down devoutly at the altar rail to receive the Body and Blood of the Lord on the tongue, as with paten in hand the gaze of the minister or acolyte accompanies the motions of the priest, anxious that every piece be collected and consumed. The whole *Vetus Ordo* is a splendid profession of faith in the mystery of transubstantiation, which only the genius of St Thomas Aquinas could illuminate with notions of extraordinary beauty, such as the arguments from fittingness presented in the *Summa Theologiae* (III, q. 73, a. 5), or with expressions drenched in the sweetest poetry, like the Eucharistic hymns he composed for the solemnity of Corpus Christi.

To rein in the action of the devil — now *that* is pastoral work! — to put his legions to flight, to block his malignant influence over persons, especially believers, over places, over things, there is need of Masses, many Masses, offered to God with faith, devotion, recollection, all the spiritual qualities that the *Vetus Ordo* encourages. Yes, dear Friends, for the good of souls, this Mass must be promoted and spread far and wide. The devil, who was defeated on the Cross by Our Lord whose Heart was united to the Mother Co-Redemptrix, unable to accomplish anything against God and against His Mother, has flung himself against the Church who, for her defense and victory, must gather herself anew at Calvary and renew that Sacrifice whose Blood put the angel of death to flight, as the Fathers of the Church have taught us, commenting typologically and allegorically on the events of the Old Testament. The Tridentine Mass communicates in a supple way, without digressing into worldviews alien to the Catholic faith, that every Mass is essentially the unbloody re-presentation of that one Sacrifice.

Speaking of the Fathers, there is one teaching I would like to recall. St Ignatius of Antioch, a very ancient Father from the beginning of the second century, probably a disciple of St John, declares that God works His miracles in silence because there they are hidden from the devil.[6] Isn't it beautiful that the words of the Canon are pronounced by the priest entirely in a low voice while a hieratic silence envelops time? It all remains hidden to the Devil, who is furiously put to flight by the august Sacrament, with the hatred and anger of one who has been cast down and defeated, which sometimes manifests in possessed souls liberated at the very moment of Consecration.

SPREADING THE *VETUS ORDO*:
A SPIRITUAL WORK OF MERCY

Desperate times call for desperate measures. Let's begin our response with the Mass. Through the spread of the

---

6   Ignatius of Antioch, *Letter to the Ephesians*, 19.

extraordinary form, we can help restore the dignity, sacrality, and beauty that souls need in order to grow in an authentic Eucharistic spirituality, whose benefits cannot be numbered, as St Pio of Pietrelcina said to Cleonice Morcaldi. This work of spreading the Tridentine Mass is a comprehensive and multifaceted work of spiritual mercy because it educates minds, comforts the pains of the afflicted, corrects sinners, gives light in times of doubt and crisis of every kind, and is a supremely powerful prayer for the living and the dead. Among its fruits is sanctification, which means pardoning those who offend us, patience and meekness toward those who vex us. Spiritual works of mercy are extremely urgent.[7] Cardinal Biffi, that great pastor of the Italian Church, made this observation twenty years ago:

> The Lord Jesus makes Himself present in our churches
> under the Eucharistic signs to show us that there is no
> truly Christian and ecclesial act of attention to others

7 Pope Francis has spoken authoritatively about the spiritual works of mercy: "It is my burning desire that, during this Jubilee, the Christian people may reflect on the *corporal and spiritual works of mercy*. It will be a way to reawaken our conscience, too often grown dull in the face of poverty. And let us enter more deeply into the heart of the Gospel where the poor have a special experience of God's mercy. Jesus introduces us to these works of mercy in his preaching so that we can know whether or not we are living as his disciples. Let us rediscover these corporal works of mercy: to feed the hungry, give drink to the thirsty, clothe the naked, welcome the stranger, heal the sick, visit the imprisoned, and bury the dead. And let us not forget the spiritual works of mercy: to counsel the doubtful, instruct the ignorant, admonish sinners, comfort the afflicted, forgive offences, bear patiently those who do us ill, and pray for the living and the dead." Francis, *Misericordiae Vultus*, accessible at http://w2.vatican.va/content/francesco/en/apost_letters/documents/papa-francesco_bolla_20150411_misericordiae-vultus.html.

that does not draw its force, its power, its justification from Him; to show us that we cannot ever separate even mentally our initiatives of solidarity from that personal relationship of love with Him who inspires and qualifies them all; to show us that the great danger of Christianity in our times is to be reduced step by step, perhaps through a generous concern to agree with everyone, to a collection of humanitarian works and the exaltation of values that are "sellable" in the global market. He dwells truly, really, corporally in the midst of us and awaits us, as the great and true dispenser of every mercy: the mercy of the truth against the snares of deceptive ideologies; the mercy of certainty against the culture of doubt; the mercy that indicates where good is and where evil is, against the many confusions in which we have been plunged; the mercy of joy that overcomes all sadness; the mercy of forgiveness for all our faults, great and small; the mercy of patience with us, notwithstanding our sinfulness and ineffectiveness; the mercy of a faithful pontiff (Heb 2:12) who intercedes for us. On the altar and in the tabernacle "we do not have a high priest who is unable to sympathize with our weaknesses, but we have one who in every respect has been tested as we are, yet without sin." So let us approach the throne of grace with full confidence, to receive mercy, find grace, and be helped in times of need. [8]

8 G. Biffi, "Eucaristia e opere di misericordia," Congresso eucaristico di Siena, June 3, 1994, www.bastabugie.it/it/articoli.php?id=3166.

There is the tightest of bonds linking spiritual works of mercy with the Holy Mass, altar, and tabernacle, as Cardinal Biffi said and as the ancient rite expresses so luminously. As we receive benefits from this work of mercy that Our Lord dispenses for us and for all, let me recommend that we become apostles and missionaries in the following way. Before those who are opposed to the Tridentine Mass, let us present a clear and solid argumentation, peacefully and politely, starting always from the reasons held by the other, accompanying him and helping him to appreciate our own reasons, mindful of what St Francis de Sales said: "There is no religious question that cannot be solved between persons of good intention."

Let us take care that celebrations of the *Vetus Ordo* are regular and dignified: they speak for themselves; they strike and attract those whom we invite to it, as circumstances allow, with gentleness and apostolic zeal. Let everything be done without worry of success and without fears of failure. The Lord asks us to do everything, but only the everything that we are capable of, and He will take care of the rest. Given the evils in the world and in the Church, it is always He and He alone who prepares the triumph of the Immaculate Heart of Mary, during whose apparition at Fatima an angel taught us to say: "I believe in You, I adore You, I hope in You, I love you." Which is what we do in every Holy Mass: we believe, we adore, we hope, and we love the supremely loveable God.

−4−
Liturgical Latin
AN IMMATERIAL PATRIMONY[†]

Eminent professors and students, dear friends,

IN THE LECTURE I AM ABOUT TO deliver on the subject that was entrusted to me, I will develop three points. First, I will define the concept of immaterial patrimony and apply it to the Latin language. Second, I will demonstrate a few characteristics of liturgical Latin. Finally, I will present the so-called "Tridentine Mass," also commonly identified as the "Latin Mass," as a rite that gives a distinguished place to liturgical Latin.

THE CONCEPT OF IMMATERIAL PATRIMONY

In order to define the concept of an immaterial patrimony, I would like to refer to an initiative promoted two and a half years ago by a worthy Italian cultural institution, the Academy "Vivarium Novum," that together with other prestigious European partners has gathered very substantial support to encourage the United Nations to declare the Latin and ancient Greek languages "an immaterial cultural patrimony of humanity." In the petition that was circulated, an immaterial patrimony of humanity was described (using other words) as any intangible spiritual good capable of creating diachronic communion between the people who make use of it. Like all cultural riches,

† A LECTURE GIVEN IN MILAN, MAY 2014.

it represents a significant experience of the human journey that can touch the soul of man as such, without exclusions and across barriers of time and space.

This category includes languages — even those never and/ or no longer spoken by a particular people — that have played a fundamental role in the history of ideas and culture. There are numerous examples. Sanskrit has, especially in India, transmitted doctrine and philosophical speculations from the most remote epochs down to our own day. Classical Arabic and medieval Persian have given us the meditations of Sufi mystics and discussions of thinkers who reflected profoundly upon their sacred texts and the works of Greek philosophy. The Hebrew language, recently brought back to life with the birth of the State of Israel, has for nearly two millennia transmitted the religious wisdom of a community of believers dispersed across the globe. These and other languages, and the civilizations they represent, constitute a grand patrimony that deserves our respect, esteem, and protection. If these are lost or neglected, everyone is culturally impoverished, which is equivalent to saying that the humanity of everyone is impoverished.[1]

It is abundantly clear that the concept of immaterial patrimony as just described can be applied to the Latin and Greek languages. Who could deny that the historical roots and the inexhaustible treasure of the common memory of Europe reside principally in the Greek and Latin civilizations?

Latin is an immortal patrimony of humanity because it is the language of the authors we define as "classic." As Italo Calvino happily observed, every time we enter into dialogue with them,

1 Cf. "An appeal to Unesco on behalf of the Latin and Greek 'heritage of humanity.'"

we always discover something new that inscribes itself in our souls.[2] It is for this reason that Virgil, with his dolorous meditation on human events, and Seneca, who maintained that all people have the same dignity, and Augustine, who in his agonizing yet serene autobiography discovered depth psychology, are all classics. There is no need to go on naming the Latin "classics" and their imperishable message. Instead, I would like to recall that, after the fall of the Western Roman Empire, accompanied in the fifth century by the influx of new peoples, the Latin language became immortal, destined never again to die. Beginning in the fifth century, civil and political communities selected Latin for their daily conversations, to be the basis of relationships, for drawing up administrative acts, for composing literary works, and for the celebration of prayers. In this way the peoples of Europe, in dialogue with one another through the use of the same language, developed a unique spirit of their own. Also writing in Latin, the educated monks of Charlemagne's palatine court cultivated humanistic studies and precipitated a renaissance of letters and the arts — Alcuin most notable among them. The devout doctors of the Middle Ages composed their *summae* of theology in Latin, to show the way by which men could understand the mysteries of the Christian faith with rational arguments. We think especially of the greatest among them, Thomas Aquinas. In Latin as well, Dante Alighieri, like others of his contemporaries, treated problems of a political nature. In Latin the humanists of the fifteenth and sixteenth centuries exalted the grandeur and dignity of man: Erasmus of Rotterdam, the prophet of peace; or Thomas More, martyr for justice. Others used Latin, such as Francesco de Vittoria, the

2   Cf. Italo Calvino, *Perché leggere i classici* (Milano: Mondadori, 1995).

great philosopher of Salamanca who fought to vindicate the inviolable rights of the indigenous populations against the greed of the conquistadors. Other renowned scholars delved deeply into mathematics, such as John Napier, who in the sixteenth century wrote a work entitled *Mirifici Logarithmorum Canonis Descriptio*.[3] How many masterpieces of literature, philosophy, theology, law, science, mathematics, and biology were composed in this language, even down to the nineteenth century! Even in the political realm, Latin was the language of the parliaments of Croatia and Hungary until the nineteenth century, and the language of correspondence between learned men, merchants, explorers, and missionaries: an enormous patrimony, truly universal in its reach across time and space.

LATIN AS A SACRED LANGUAGE IN THE CATHOLIC CHURCH

Of all the contexts in which the Latin language has been used, far and away the most distinguished is the liturgy of the Catholic Church, which in the West almost spontaneously chose the language of Rome as a means to lift its prayer to God in her most solemn acts, the sacraments, and especially the Holy Mass and the Divine Office. Among the various causes that contributed to this felicitous symbiosis between the official prayer of the Church and the use of Latin, I would like to note one in particular: that Latin is a sacred language. The arguments I adduce to support this thesis are five.

First, the earliest examples of Latin's literary use, the extremely ancient *carmina*, were ritual texts. The phonetic

3 Cf. Roberto Spataro, *Hortensius vel Sapientia veterum a Christi-fidelibus tradita* (Grottaminarda: Delta, 2014), 81.

characteristics of Latin, with its alternation of long and short syllables, with the robust but never ungraceful sonority created by occlusive consonants, refined by the frequency of sibilants and liquids, make it a poetic language. Rising above mere functionality in its prose, Latin moves in the sphere of the beautiful, which is the world of God.

Further, Latin is a "sacred" language because, as Michael Lang has noted following Christine Mohrmann, it is immutable.[4] In fact, the Latin language was fixed once and for all in its morphological and syntactic structures by the fifth century after Christ, experiencing only a gradual and fruitful lexical enrichment afterwards.

A sacred language, moreover, is disposed to receive loan words from other languages in order to express sacred realities, and liturgical Latin showed itself very pliable at this time in receiving Grecisms and Hebraisms.

The sacred language has a rhetorical structure typical of orality, which contributes to its majesty and beauty. It suffices to read any oration in the Roman Missal to discover a rhetorical elaboration perfect in its sobriety: chiasms, hyperbatons, alliterations, perfect equilibrium of parts, and a care in the formation of clauses yielding a rhythm that is unmistakable.

There is one more clear reason that makes liturgical Latin a sacred language. The liturgical texts are crafted as an echo of and deep meditation upon the sacred text, the Bible. If one is interested in turning toward God, certainly the most appropriate

---

4 U. Michael Lang, "Il latino come lingua liturgica del Rito Romano," intervention at the First Conference on the Motu Proprio *Summorum Pontificum,* Rome, September 16–18, 2008; cf. idem, *The Voice of the Church at Prayer: Reflections on Liturgy and Language* (San Francisco: Ignatius Press, 2012).

words are those that God Himself, in His revelation, placed in the mouths of adoring believers. So now, the Catholic Church has taken up for her life, for her prayer, and for her doctrine the Vulgate, the Latin edition of the Bible, written by Jerome in the fourth century and amended after the Council of Trent.

LATIN IN THE TRIDENTINE MASS

Having established that Latin is an immaterial patrimony of humanity and that, among its various forms and expressions, there exists a *liturgical* Latin which is the sacred form of the Latin language, I would like to address a question that has probably occurred to someone among us: hasn't the Catholic Church, with the introduction of the national languages following the postconciliar liturgical reform, abandoned the use of Latin in the celebration of the liturgy? The problem is complex. I present three elements that help to address the problem properly.

First of all, it should be recalled that the Fathers of the Second Vatican Council permitted a limited and reasonable use of the national languages to coexist beside Latin.[5] The reasons why

5   Cf. Sacrum Concilium Oecumenicum Vaticanum II, *Sacrosanctum Concilium*, n. 36, in *Constitutiones, Decreta, Declarationes,* cura et studio Secretariae Generalis Concilii Oecumenici Vaticani II (Rome: Typis Poliglottis Vaticanis, 1966). "§ 1. Particular law remaining in force, the use of the Latin language is to be preserved in the Latin rites. § 2. But since the use of the mother tongue, whether in the Mass, the administration of the sacraments, or other parts of the liturgy, frequently may be of great advantage to the people, the limits of its employment may be extended. This will apply in the first place to the readings and directives, and to some of the prayers and chants, according to the regulations on this matter to be laid down separately in subsequent chapters." Cf. n. 54: "In Masses which are celebrated with the people, a suitable place may be allotted to their mother tongue. This is to apply in the first place to the readings and the 'common prayer,' but also, as local conditions may warrant, to those

this recommendation was disrespected and overlooked must be clarified by historians.

Secondly, all *editiones typicæ* of the liturgical texts are still in Latin. The texts in national languages have been translated from the original Latin, an operation that has proved very delicate, since the faith of the Church is at stake — so delicate that the Holy See reserves to itself the right to approve all such translations before they are introduced in practice. Of the infinite problems of translations, I would like to cite two examples. At the beginning of the Mass, whether in the *forma ordinaria* or *forma extraordinaria*, the *Confiteor* is recited, albeit with some not irrelevant variations between the one and the other. This very beautiful prayer concludes with an address of the faithful to the Church Triumphant and Militant, asking them to pray that they may obtain the forgiveness of their sins. In Latin it says: "Ideo precor . . . orare pro me ad Dominum Deum nostrum." The Italian language translation says: "Supplico di pregare per me il Signore Dio nostro," the English "to pray for me to the Lord our God." But the Latin preposition "ad" indicates more than merely a sense of direction, as in the English translation "to the Lord our God." Rather, an accusative in dependence on a verb that does not indicate movement, such as *confiteor*, means principally "in the presence of." Thus, when the Confiteor is

---

parts which pertain to the people, according to the norm laid down in Art. 36 of this Constitution. Nevertheless steps should be taken so that the faithful may also be able to say or to sing together in Latin those parts of the Ordinary of the Mass which pertain to them." In n. 101 we read: "In accordance with the centuries-old tradition of the Latin rite, the Latin language is to be retained by clerics in the Divine Office. But in individual cases the ordinary has the power of granting the use of a vernacular translation to those clerics for whom the use of Latin constitutes a grave obstacle to their praying the office properly."

recited, we place ourselves "in the presence of God." In the Mass we are truly before Him, as sinners, all of us, and we invoke His pardon because we are in the sight of Him who underwent His Passion and death to pardon us. (The position of the crucifix also helps us to assume this interior orientation.)

Even more surprising is the Italian language translation of the words of consecration over the chalice: "Accipite et bibite ex eo omnes: Hic est enim calix sanguinis mei, novi et aeterni testamenti." The translation of the Italian Missal reads: "Questo è il sangue per la nuova ed eterna alleanza," a complement of purpose and not of specification: "This is the blood *for* the new and eternal covenant." The translation is absolutely inadequate: in the place of an objective-constitutive genitive (this is the blood that "makes," creates, constitutes the new and definitive covenant), there is a much weaker complement "per la nuova ed eterna alleanza." At this point, the *lex orandi* does not correspond to the *lex credendi*.

The supreme Magisterium of the Church has never ceased to encourage the use of the Latin language even in the reformed liturgy. In this regard, the example and teaching of Pope Emeritus Benedict XVI were luminous.

However, I would now like to offer some reflections on the form of celebration of the Mass in which the use of the Latin language has remained whole and intact, the so-called *forma extraordinaria* of the Roman rite according to the Missal of 1962, which, with the Motu Proprio *Summorum Pontificum*, has been restored to the Church, and which a number of faithful and priests, albeit extremely small in respect to the majority, have permanently adopted.[6]

6 Benedictus XVI, *Litterae Apostolicae Motu proprio datae Summorum Pontificum*, July 7, 2007.

The Tridentine Mass — so we may call it — strongly accentuates the sacrality of the ritual action as an act of faith that we can summarize in this manner: God is most really and truly present through the consecration of the Eucharistic species, and in the Mass the sacrifice of Calvary is renewed in an unbloody manner. Faced with an event so sublime, the priest and the faithful are asked to cultivate an attitude of intimate and firm belief, of silent adoration, of humble welcome, of recollected prayer. The Latin language, as a sacred language, lends itself excellently to creating this atmosphere. Christine Mohrmann, a great historian of Christian Latin, argues that a sacred language is a specific way to "organize" religious experience. In fact, every form of belief in supernatural reality or the existence of a transcendent being leads necessarily to the adoption of a form of sacred language in worship, while only a radical anti-clericalism leads to rejecting every form of sacred language. Further, in their acts of worship almost all the great religions adopt a language different from the one used for daily speech. Cardinal Ranjith recalled this in an interview some years ago:

> The use of a sacred language is a tradition across the whole world. In Hinduism the language of prayer is Sanskrit, which is no longer in daily use. In Buddhism Pali is used, a language that only Buddhist monks study today. In Islam the Arabic of the Qur'an is employed. The use of a sacred language helps us to live the sense of the transcendent.[7]

7 Marco Politi, "Liturgia. Perché Ratzinger recupera il 'sacro,'" in *La Repubblica*, July 31, 2008, p. 42.

In a conference held at Pavia a little over a year ago, Dom Marino Neri, a passionate devotee of the Tridentine Mass, explained that Latin conduces better to the sense of mystery in the moment when the supremely Other is sensibly communicated to us. This alterity, expressed in places, gestures, vestments, also runs through the "prince" of signs, the word, which not only mediates meaning destined for the intellect, but leads those present into the personal religious relationship that is nourished by signs. In short, we are dealing with a principle formulated by St Thomas Aquinas, the theologian who says the most reasonable things I have ever discovered: "What is found in the sacraments through human institution is not necessary for the validity of the sacrament, but confers a certain solemnity, useful for exciting devotion and reverence in those who receive them."[8]

In addition to the sacrality of the Tridentine Rite, most powerfully and effectively manifested in the use of the hieratic language of Latin, we may point to further characteristics in symbiotic harmony with it that make the extraordinary form of the Roman rite an authentic mystical experience. I note three of them briefly. They are well known to those who have participated at least a few times, or who habitually assist at the old Mass. First and foremost, the position assumed by the faithful and celebrants encourages an orientation *ad Deum*. Rejecting the rather self-referential circle of "presence to one another," they turn their gaze toward the crucifix, so majestic and simple in the salvific message it conveys: the Blood of Christ, shed violently on Calvary, is shed in an unbloody manner on the altar where the Holy Sacrifice is renewed.

8 *Summa Theologiae* III, q. 64, a. 2 (ed. Leonina).

Secondly, the space given to silence, which discreetly enfolds the whole progress of the rite from the priestly preparations to the recitation of the *Canon Missae*, and gives emphasis to contemplation and intimate assimilation of the meaning of the gestures performed and the words pronounced. Finally, the third characteristic, the importance of gestures that, in the logic proper to symbols, sum up Christian anthropology, inviting the faithful to be frequently on their knees so as to recognize their creaturely condition before the Creator who loves and saves them, and who neglects no dimension of the life of man, not even the sentiments he directs toward the altar — that eloquent figure of Christ, Himself the victim, priest, and altar — which the priest repeatedly kisses with such tenderness.

I conclude with one example of the beauty of liturgical Latin, a significant part of this immaterial patrimony of humanity. It is a prayer that the priest pronounces softly at the end of the Mass before imparting the final blessing. Unfortunately it is not found in the *forma ordinaria* of the Roman rite. He recites it this way:

> Placeat tibi, sancta Trinitas, obsequium servitutis meae: et praesta, ut sacrificium, quod oculis tuae maiestatis indignus obtuli, tibi sit acceptabile, mihique et omnibus, pro quibus illud obtuli, sit, te miserante, propitiabile. Per Christum Dominum nostrum. Amen.[9]

---

9 "May the homage of my bounden duty be pleasing to Thee, O Holy Trinity; and grant that the sacrifice which I, though unworthy, have offered in the sight of Thy Majesty may be acceptable to Thee, and through Thy mercy be a propitiation for me and for all those for whom I have offered it. Through Christ our Lord. Amen."

In this prayer, heaven and earth are united in the words of the priest: the Trinity invoked at the beginning of the prayer and all the faithful for whom the priest prays and works. The subjunctive *placeat* alternates with the imperative *praesta*, which are the verbal modes of Christian prayer: when we speak to God we express a humble hope, and thus the subjunctive, but we also dare to ask in faith, in the name of the Son, and thus the imperative. The requests are expressed in order: first the glory of God, in the proposition "ut sacrificium sit acceptabile," and then the salvation of souls, "sit propitiabile," the same arrangement as the Lord's Prayer, the Our Father. The prayers are expressed in an elegant parallelism that is broken by an ablative absolute, a typical Latin construction expressing the circumstances that accompany an action or thought. Breaking from the parallel structure, this ablative absolute intrudes itself as a sort of light that illuminates the whole prayer: "te miserante," suggestive of the very motto chosen by Pope Francis:[10] the mercy of the Three Persons of the Most Holy Trinity, the imperishable message of the Gospel that the current Supreme Pontiff unceasingly reminds us about and that the Tridentine Mass, restored to us by Benedictus Magnus, leads us to at the conclusion of every celebration!

---

10 Miserando atque eligendo.

−5−
Latin and the Church's Magisterium[†]

Dear Friends,

I AM VERY GRATEFUL TO THE ORGA-
nizers of this initiative for the chance to address such
a qualified audience as yourselves about the reasons
that have led the Catholic Church to adopt the Latin
language as the official language of her Magisterium
and to maintain this decision to the present day.

Before entering *in medias res*, I would like to spell out what
genres of documents the Holy See publishes in Latin.[1] In the
first place, the papal *litterae encyclicae* and the post-synodal
adhortationes apostolicae, which have a very prominent role
among papal documents, are published in Latin. Through
them the successors of Peter express their ordinary and universal
Magisterium in order to promote and defend the spiritual and
doctrinal life of the Church. Latin is used for the *epistulae apostolicae*, which deal with specific topics relating to doctrine and
pastoral life, such as *Mane nobiscum Domine* of St John Paul II,
composed on the occasion of the Year of the Eucharist, and for
the *litterae decretales* published in the event of canonizations.

1 For this introductory part, see W. Turk, *Il latino dei documenti
pontifici e della Curia Romana*, in M. Sodi, E. dal Covolo, *Il latino e i cris-
tiani. Un bilancio all'inizio del terzo millennio* (Vatican City, 2012), 273–91.

† A LECTURE GIVEN IN PAVIA, FEBRUARY 2013.

The *constitutiones apostolicae*, documents of ancient tradition in the Roman Curia, used either for solemn decisions such as the promulgation of the Roman Missal, or for events more frequent in the life of the Church such as the erection of a diocese, are in Latin. Also written in the Latin language are the *brevia apostolica* for the beatification of a servant of God or the erection of a religious institute.[2]

Though they do not relate to the Magisterium *stricto sensu*, I would like to point out that the Apostolic See responds in Latin to ambassadors who present their letters of credence, and in Latin the apostolic nuncios present their credentials to the countries where they perform their services. It is also customary to write the letters, signed by the Holy Father, that commemorate the anniversary of the priestly and episcopal ordinations of bishops, in Latin.

The monthly *Acta Apostolicae Sedis*, the official bulletin of the acts of the Holy See, is published in Latin and one need only open a number of the *Commentarii* to realize the percentage of documents drafted in Latin. Among the magisterial texts of greater importance in the life of the Church, including the Acts of the Second Vatican Ecumenical Council, the *Codex Iuris Canonici*, and the *Catechismus Catholicae Ecclesiae*, the official editions are always in Latin.

Ecclesiastical Latin is quite elegant, extremely precise from a morphological and syntactic point of view, modeled on the graceful movements of the classical style, but at the same time not overly complicated in structure and vocabulary. Benedict XVI's Motu Proprio *Latina Lingua*, by which he established

2 In English, these documents are called, respectively: encyclical letters; apostolic exhortations; apostolic letters; decretal letters; apostolic constitutions; apostolic briefs.

the *Pontificia Academia Latinitatis*, after affirming that Latin is the language of the *editio typica* of the liturgical books of the Roman rite, reiterates this option in favor of Latin: "In hac lingua…, praestantiora Magisterii pontificii documenta necnon sollemniora Romanorum Pontificum officialia Acta."[3] After this introduction, I will carry out the rest of my talk in two points: first, Latin assures the universality of ecclesial teaching; second, Latin assures its immutability.

LATIN ASSURES UNIVERSALITY

The Magisterium of the Holy See is addressed to the episcopate and the faithful of the whole Catholic world. Hence it is necessary to employ a language that is "neutral" or, as I prefer to say, "supranational."[4] A national language, even one whose use is widespread, is tied to the people or peoples whose language is used, and inevitably ends up spreading their particular culture, which lacks that universality that is an essential character of the supreme Magisterium of the Church. The modern languages are rooted in the geographical and cultural terrain in which they were born and develop over time. Inevitably, they threaten always to introduce a process of linguistic-cultural colonization, imposing their particular *Weltanschauung* along with the language, since no language is a simple neutral instrument but is

3 Benedict XVI, *Latina Lingua*, 2: "In addition, precisely in order to highlight the Church's universal character, the liturgical books of the Roman rite, the most important documents of the papal magisterium, and the most solemn official acts of the Roman pontiffs are written in this language in their authentic form." http://w2.vatican.va/content/benedict-xvi/la/motu_proprio/documents/hf_ben-xvi_motu-proprio_20121110_latina-lingua.html.

4 On the following reflexions, see Roberto Jacoangeli, "Il 'Pontificium Institutum Altioris Latinitatis,'" in *Salesianum* XXVI (1964): 231–55.

always the vector for a culture. In this vein I would like to cite the thought of a great jurist and sociologist, one of the glories of the Society of Jesus, Father Luigi Taparelli (1793–1862):

> A Church that embraces all peoples of the world needs a universal language, but it has no pretext for adopting one language over another: any preference would be an injustice.... On the human level the Church needs a universal language, unchanging and intellectual, that rescues her from a choice detrimental to her unity.[5]

This concept is also formulated in two papal documents exalting the worth of the Latin language: the letter *Officiorum Omnium* of Pope Pius XI which appeared in 1922, and the well-known Apostolic Constitution of Pope John XXIII, *Veterum Sapientia* of 1962.

Unlike the spoken languages, Latin possesses the character of synchronic universality. This property derives from its diachronic universality. I mean to say that within and outside of the Church, Latin has been employed for centuries as the lingua franca *par excellence* of educated persons and in contexts calling for a communication unfettered by national linguistic forms. After the fall of the Western Roman Empire, whose inhabitants used Latin as their official language, Latin was used for many more centuries from northern Europe to North Africa, from the Iberian peninsula to the Balkans, as a living language for writing and speaking. We may consider for a moment the long and luminous centuries of the Middle Ages, centuries in which

5 Luigi Taparelli, *Saggio teoretico di Diritto Naturale appoggiato sul fatto* (Rome, 1835), 2:436–38.

the universities were born. We can think of humanism from Petrarch to Erasmus of Rotterdam. In these ages and beyond, cultivated men born in various countries and having different cultural customs felt they belonged to the same *res publica litterarum* and engaged in peaceful and fruitful dialogue with one another using the Latin language, without German or French or Italian, also rich living languages, being able to succeed in imposing its own vision of things.

Latin is truly a universal language and the Church, a catholic institution by her very name, made and still makes use of it to spread her official teaching in all pronouncements of major importance. Furthermore, between Latin and the Catholic Church a certain connaturality, a spontaneous friendship, has grown up. Indeed, the Roman Church's ever-expanding exercise of its universal Magisterium has gone hand in hand with the privileging of Latin — the language employed, as I have just said, by men of culture, the language in which theological treatises were composed and the greater part of works of spirituality, the legislation of canon law, and the liturgical books. This treasure has been and still is the source of ecclesial teaching. There thus exists a vital relationship between the Latin of the documents of the Magisterium and the Latin of a vast intra-ecclesial literary heritage: a patrimony that has burgeoned without ceasing and, as it accumulated, became the linguistic *humus* of the Magisterium of the Holy See.

Now I move on to a corollary to the argument I have just developed. If the Church were to abandon Latin in the presentation of the most important acts of her Magisterium, it would amount to a very dangerous decision, not merely on a cultural level but also from an ecclesiological point of view. It would be a *vulnus* (wound) to her essential property of unity — "credo

Ecclesiam unam catholicam"[6] — in favor of a particularist eccle-siological vision in which the Catholic Church would become a federation of local churches. It is not merely by chance that those who have demonstrated their indifference or even hostility toward the use of Latin in the Church have also been advocates for weakening the Petrine primacy and for the radicalization of episcopal collegiality, propositions with extremely danger-ous consequences. Among the enemies of Latin throughout the history of the Church can be counted, for example, the Christian denominations born in the age of the Reformation, which have dramatically ruptured the unity of the *Catholica* in western Europe.

Yes, the Magisterium of the Catholic Church needs a truly universal language! And Latin corresponds to this imperative in a noble and admirable manner.

LATIN ASSURES IMMUTABILITY

Latin is graced with a second property, closely related to the one I have just explained. Latin is an immutable language, as authoritatively defined by the two documents I recalled above, *Officiorum Omnium* and *Veterum Sapientia*. In John XXIII's apostolic constitution we read the following: "Lingua Latina, iamdiu adversus varietates tuta, quas cotidiana populi consue-tudo in vocabulorum notionem inducere solet, fixa quidem censenda est et immobilis."[7] Indeed, more or less since the fall

---

6 "I believe in one catholic (i.e., universal) Church."

7 "The Latin language is set and unchanging. It has long since ceased to be affected by those alterations in the meaning of words which are the normal result of daily, popular use." John XXIII, *Veterum Sapientia* 6, https://w2.vatican.va/content/john-xxiii/la/apost_constitutions/1962/documents/hf_j-xxiii_apc_19620222_veterum-sapientia.html.

of the Roman Empire in the West, the process of transformation that marks other languages was substantially arrested in Latin. Though used in a living way for many centuries and by many persons in diverse contexts, as noted above, it attained a stable syntactic structure and morphology, even as it continued to witness a moderate lexical enrichment tied to the evolution of technology, arts, science, law, and morals, in short, of life itself.

This solidification of the language into well-defined registers gave Latin the ability to express concepts with clarity and strength of thought. Latin therefore offered itself as the most valid language for all those domains of knowledge and human communication in which certainty, force of expression, precision, and richness of nuance were desired. This is why it was for centuries the preferred language of scientists and jurists, philologists and musicians, and, in the ambit of the Catholic Church, the language of the Magisterium, especially on dogmatic subjects where no ambiguity or obscurity may be admitted.

One hundred years ago, another saint, Pope Pius X — and we must heed the saints — declared that the Latin language is suitable for expressing in the clearest and most felicitous manner the most difficult concepts and the most subtle aspects of human reasoning. Without insisting too much on the efficacy of Latin as if it were a divine idiom, I believe Pius's claim must not be underrated. But whence comes this efficacy?

Latin is a very sober language. It uses a few words to express a concept that requires many words in modern languages. And when many words are used, the risk of conflicting interpretations grows. Latin tends to concreteness and is less inclined to bold abstractions. In this way its thinking is, in a certain sense, more trustworthy. Certain texts of theology — a type of ecclesial magisterium not institutional and authoritative but scientific and charismatic — are full of words and concepts that flow in a redundant stream, and manage to complicate rather than simplify the communication of thought. Of course I am not saying it is necessary to write in Latin, but if theologians knew Latin well — and they cannot avoid knowing it since the major part of the sources of their discipline is written in this language — they would be habituated to a discipline of word and thought that, frankly, seems to be mostly absent today.

Latin is endowed with its own *perspicuitas* whereby each element of the *circuitus* has a logical and syntactic function that confers clarity in communication. When one wants to assert definitive truths, albeit with the humility proper to human thought, Latin serves very well. And thus, if I may be permitted to use a metaphor, the Latin period is like a spy story or a thriller: one must read a period to the last word and then, proceeding through clues (here the subject, here the predicate, here the object, here the conjugations that create the relations between words and the *cola* of the phrases), one discovers the "villain." In this way, one reconstructs the sense of the thought, which stands out firm and clear.

At this point, I would like to offer an example and show at the same time that translation, by its very nature as a linguistic operation, can never entirely communicate the contents of its Latin original. I examine the *incipit* of one of the most important documents of the Second Vatican Council and perhaps the ecclesial Magisterium of the whole 20th century: the conciliar Declaration *Dignitatis Humanae*. Let's compare the Latin and English texts as they appear at the website of the Holy See:[8]

---

8 Concilium Oecumenicum Vaticanum II, *Dignitatis Humanae*, n. 1.

Dignitatis humanae personae homines hac nostra aetate magis in dies conscii fiunt, atque numerus eorum crescit qui exigunt, ut in agendo homines proprio suo consilio et libertate responsabili fruantur et utantur, non coercitione commoti, sed officii conscientia ducti. Itemque postulant iuridicam delimitationem potestatis publicae, ne fines honestae libertatis et personae et associationum nimis circumscribantur.	A sense of the dignity of the human person has been impressing itself more and more deeply on the consciousness of contemporary man, and the demand is increasingly made that men should act on their own judgment, enjoying and making use of a responsible freedom, not driven by coercion but motivated by a sense of duty. The demand is likewise made that constitutional limits should be set to the powers of government, in order that there may be no encroachment on the rightful freedom of the person and of associations.

First of all, one notices that the Latin text is more concise: as we said, its sobriety confers greater force, where the modern languages are more verbose and so more open to interpretations. Further, only one who reads it in Latin knows that a Latin text gives great importance to the first words of the period, which it can allow thanks to declensions that clarify each word's syntactic function, as opposed to English which is obliged to place the subject at the head of the phrase. The first words of the text are "dignitatis humanae"; thus in Latin we immediately understand the key to reading the whole document: the dignity of the human person, which justifies the development of the Magisterium on the theme of religious liberty. Another consideration: the English translation has preferred an abstraction ("a sense," "the demand"), but the reader of the original text notices instead the historical role of peoples: "homines, eorum numerus." And why translate the very concrete term "conscientia officii" with "a sense of duty"?

I conclude with what is perhaps a marginal observation. There is one more reason Latin is well adapted, in my mind, to magisterial pronouncements. Latin is a *lingua non vulgaris*, as *Veterum Sapientia* declared, or as I like to say, it is beautiful. It is full of majesty and nobility. The Latin language is artistic. Is it possible not to admire the *concinnitas*[9] of Cicero and (though more fluid) of Livy? Or enjoy the Senecan periods that invite us to meditate on its paratactic phrases, so terse and effective? How can one not feel the thrill of beauty in the psychological depth of Augustine, expressed in that style so undeniably classic and modern, where rhetorical figures give such a unique vigor to his thought? How can we avoid comparing the style of Leo the Great to a striking and imposing architecture? And when it comes to documents of the papal Magisterium, many texts are masterpieces of style. I cite one passage from Paul VI's Encyclical Letter *Ecclesiam Suam* where the expressive force of the anaphora stretches out only to converge upon a double rhetorical question that compels rational and emotional assent:

> Caritas omnia explanat. Caritas ad recta omnia inducit. Nihil omnino est, quod per caritatem effici ac renovari nequeat. Caritas omnia suffert, omnia credit, omnia sperat, omnia sustinet. Quis nostrum haec ignoret? Quodsi haec novimus, nonne hoc tempus est caritatis exercendae?[10]

9 Harmony of style, studied elegance, flowing beauty.

10 Paul VI, *Ecclesiam Suam*, n. 2. "Charity is the key to everything. It sets all to rights. There is nothing that charity cannot achieve and renew.

Why did I bring up this property of the Latin language? Because the truth, to which the texts of the Magisterium intend to lead us and which they desire to demonstrate, is intrinsically tied to the mystery of beauty. "Ens, unum, verum, bonum, pulchrum, convertuntur,"[11] as the medieval masters taught us.

Yes, Latin is the language whose ardent apologist Pius XI readily defined as "loquendi genus pressum, locuples, numerosum, maiestatis plenum et dignitatis."[12] It is the *genus loquendi*, therefore, most appropriate to the exercise of the *munus docendi* in the Church for the good of man and the glory of God.

Charity 'beareth all things, believeth all things, hopeth all things, endureth all things.' Who is there among us who does not realize this? And since we realize it, is not this the time to put it into practice?"

11   "Being, one, true, good, beautiful, are convertible terms."

12   Pius XI, *Officiorum Omnium*, in *AAS* 14 (1922): 452–53: "a kind of speech compact, rich, rhythmic, full of majesty and dignity."

– 6 –

Benedict XVI,
"Doctor of the Church," and
the Liturgical Reform†

Honored ladies, distinguished gentlemen, dear friends,

I AM VERY GRATEFUL TO THE ORGA-
nizers of this event. I am happy to share my reflections
with you here, in the land of Tuscany, where the Association for the application of the Motu Proprio *Summorum Pontificum* works with a diligence appreciated
by so many. The title of the lecture I share with you refers to
the Pope Emeritus, whom I make bold to call a "doctor of the
Church."

In the works of her doctors, the Church recognizes a sure and
superior source of truth. In moral questions, for example, who
is better than the Doctor of the Church Alphonsus Liguori? For
the mystical life, would we hesitate to consult John of the Cross?
Benedict XVI himself proclaimed "doctors": John of Avila for
his eminent teachings on the priesthood, and Hildegard von
Bingen for her theological-symbolical science.

As we know, the title "Doctor of the Church" is conferred
on those masters of theology and spirituality who have already
been canonized and are no longer living. Nevertheless, the richness of the magisterium of Benedict XVI, the luminosity of his

† A LECTURE GIVEN IN PRATO, OCTOBER 2014.

teachings, the profundity of his analyses, and the reliability of his syntheses permit us to call him, by way of anticipation or if you will analogically, an authentic doctor to whom the Church can resort today or whenever it needs to face the crises that arise inevitably and in a certain sense providentially from within and without. Yes, Benedict XVI is the "doctor" of apologetics, of that articulation of theology that formulates the reason for our hope for those who, with their questions and objections, challenges and controversies, provoke, threaten, and attack the Christian faith.

I will argue my thesis by developing two points. Specifically, I will focus on two types of "crisis," the first from the outside, the second from within.

THE DEFENSE OF REASON

The historical-cultural context of the pontificate of Benedict XVI is what is considered "postmodernity," defined by sociologists as the "fluid society." What is the essence of postmodernity? It is the aggressive, intolerant expansion of relativism, characterized in that well-known formulation elaborated by then Cardinal Ratzinger in the *Missa pro eligendo Romano Pontifice* in 2005: the "dictatorship of relativism." According to this invasive and degenerate *mens* of thought and customs, neither absolute truth nor universal moral obligations pertaining to all exist. Everything is fluid relative to the opinions, emotions, tastes, and instincts of the individual. There is no true or false in thinking, no good and evil in the moral sphere, no just or unjust in the legislative. This relativistic vision of life, forcefully disseminated by the communications media, has a dictatorial tendency to eliminate every form of opposition through the marginalization and penalization of its adversaries. Who are its adversaries? Those who oppose its feeble thinking with their own robust thinking. Against a minimalist utilitarian ethic, they assert an ethic of values and responsibility, and to the legislators who sanction the legitimacy of evil, they object: *"Non licet tibi."*[1] Very often they pay for it with their lives, like the Precursor of our Lord. The voice of the current Pontiff, too, has been raised against relativism, as for example in a passage of his long Apostolic Exhortation *Evangelii Gaudium*, insufficiently noticed by commentators and the media.[2]

Benedict XVI identified and denounced the evil root of relativism in the distrust of reason and its cognitive powers. This Pontiff, coming from an Augustinian background, has affirmed in Thomistic terms what every person's common sense recognizes: the objectivity of the real. Beginning from this evident fact, which is anterior to and presupposed in reasoning, he has demolished relativism piece by piece, and shown with his serene and pacific argumentation, qualities of one inspired by God, that when the intelligence observes reality it discovers an internal rationality that does not depend on the subject, and is not relative to him.

For example, Benedict XVI argues that human reason, founded on the objectivity of the real and its intelligibility, perceives that there is a natural and thus objective difference of sexuality and that this objective difference is ordered toward child-bearing. Therefore *gender* theories are unacceptable, as is the justification and even exaltation of homosexuality, and any legislation permitting "marriage" between persons of the same sex. Relativism is given free reign only if reason "irrationally"

1   "It is not lawful for thee [to have thy brother's wife]": the words of St. John the Baptist to King Herod (Mk 6:18).
2   See Francis, *Evangelii Gaudium*, n. 61.

rejects its duty to recognize what precedes and determines it. And this has been happening for some time now.

No longer content merely to deny reality or to entertain an idea born from unsound thinking, relativism has become an ideology and assumed dictatorial connotations. The result, often pointed out by Benedict XVI in his historical lectures, is the tragic domination of the stronger over the weaker, as we can see especially in 20th-century totalitarian regimes. Today the dictatorship of relativism permits embryos to be manipulated and destroyed with impunity, the abortion of fetuses, especially when affected by physical deformations, and the adoption of babies by homosexual partners.

In this vein, I cite just one text of Benedict XVI — a Wednesday "catechesis," dedicated to one of the great believing intellectuals of the Middle Ages, John of Salisbury:

> According to John of Salisbury, an immutable objective truth also exists, whose origin is in God; it is accessible to human reason and concerns practical and social action. It is a natural law that must inspire human laws and political and religious authorities, so that they may promote the common good. This natural law is characterized by a property that John calls "equity," that is, the attribution to each person of his own rights. From this stem precepts that are legitimate for all peoples, and in no way can they be abrogated. This is the central thesis of *Policraticus,* the treatise of philosophy and political theology in which John of Salisbury reflects on the conditions that render government leaders just and acceptable.

Whereas other arguments addressed in this work are tied to the historical circumstances in which it was composed, the theme of the relationship between natural law and a positive juridical order, mediated by equity, is still of great importance today. In our time, in fact, especially in some countries, we are witnessing a disturbing divergence between reason, whose task is to discover the ethical values that flow from the dignity of the human person, and freedom, whose responsibility is to accept and promote them. John of Salisbury would remind us today that the only laws that are in conformity with equity are those that protect the sacredness of human life, rejecting the licitness of abortion, euthanasia, and bold genetic experimentation; laws that respect the dignity of marriage between a man and a woman, and are inspired by a correct account of the state's secularity, which always entails the safeguarding of religious freedom; laws that promote subsidiarity and solidarity at both the national and the international level. If laws are not in conformity with true equity, then the result is what John of Salisbury terms the "tyranny of princes," or, as we might say, "the dictatorship of relativism": a relativism that "does not recognize anything as definitive and whose ultimate goal consists solely of one's own ego and desires."[3]

It is no accident that this moderate and well-considered defense of human reason's role as an irreplaceable instrument for

---

3 Benedict XVI, "John of Salisbury," General Audience, December 16, 2009.

understanding reality and a compass for moral discernment has been valued by many experts in the secular world who are conscious of the disastrous consequences caused by a supine acceptance of the siren song of "weak thought," and are open to understanding the cogency of what the Pope Emeritus called "non-negotiable principles," which no excuse can justify abandoning in this historical-cultural moment.

At the same time, Benedict XVI has also explored the friendship that subsists between reason and Christian faith. It was not by mere coincidence but by providential design that the preaching of the Gospel, from its very first dawn, encountered a potent and universal expression of human reason, the Greek *logos*. Speaking of Thomas Aquinas, Benedict XVI argued:

> Faith, in fact, protects reason from any temptation to distrust its own abilities, stimulates it to be open to ever broader horizons, and keeps alive in it the search for foundations; and, when reason itself is applied to the supernatural sphere of the relationship between God and man, faith enriches its work. According to St Thomas, for example, human reason can certainly reach the affirmation of the existence of one God, but only faith, which receives divine Revelation, is able to draw from the mystery of the Love of the Triune God.
>
> Moreover, it is not only faith that helps reason. Reason, too, with its own means, can do something important for faith, doing it a threefold service that St Thomas sums up in the preface to his commentary on the *De Trinitate* of Boethius: "demonstrating those truths that are preambles of the faith; giving a clearer notion, by certain similitudes, of the truths of

the faith; resisting those who speak against the faith, either by showing that their statements are false, or by showing that they are not necessarily true" (q. 2, a. 3). The entire history of theology is basically the exercise of this task of the mind, which shows the intelligibility of faith, its articulation and inner harmony, its reasonableness and its ability to further human good.[4]

In his memorable Regensburg Address of September 12, 2006, Pope Benedict, with characteristic discretion and humility, invited Islam to reflect upon this point. He noted, prudently and even prophetically, that without a dialogue between faith and reason, religion can devolve into fideism and give in to the temptation to violence, which is always irrational.

THE REFORM OF THE LITURGY

On this point, too, Benedict XVI towers eminent. With unparalleled clarity, even before his elevation to the papacy, he had located the heart of Christianity's crisis in the crisis of the liturgy.

What does the liturgical crisis consist in? In the promethean attempt to construct a liturgy of human proportions, one that thinks it is speaking to God, but is really a monologue of man and his religious assembly, proudly and often ridiculously self-referential. The liturgy is for its part the authentic act of faith in which the Christian community, in devout and recollected attention, perceives the voice of God and surrenders itself to be formed by His action, the divine grace. Several practices and

---

4   Benedict XVI, "San Tommaso d'Aquino (2)," General Audience, June 16, 2010.

orientations that followed the liturgical reform after the Second Vatican Council — but not caused by the Council — have obeyed this anthropocentric logic. Thus there has arisen the need for a correction, a reorientation *ad Deum*. Benedict XVI argued for and exemplified a style of liturgical celebration in which "sacrality" was gradually restored to the faithful. He promulgated several documents of crucial importance, such as the Apostolic Exhortation *Sacramentum Caritatis*, too quickly forgotten.

But his most courageous and consequential act relating to the liturgical crisis was, it seems to me, the Motu Proprio *Summorum Pontificum*. We would be mistaken to consider it merely as an act of generosity by the Supreme Pontiff to meet the spiritual needs of a minority group of priests and faithful. On the contrary, it is an invitation to the whole Church. Knowledge, diffusion, and practice of the Holy Mass and the other sacraments in the extraordinary form is a great opportunity to restore spiritual profundity to Catholicism. This is the true pastoral priority, over and above transient circumstances. God grant it may come to pass!

For Benedict XVI, the *Vetus Ordo* is a *schola liturgica* that, when placed side by side with the *Novus Ordo*, becomes a sensitive educator that draws out all the positive potential contained in Paul VI's Missal. In the same way, the *Novus Ordo* can improve the celebration of the *Vetus Ordo* by enriching it with some sensibilities typical to the ordinary form of the Roman rite.[5]

In other words, the exquisite liturgical sensibility promoted by the Tridentine Missal not only contributes to the celebration

5   See Benedict XVI, "Letter to the Bishops on the occasion of the publication of the Apostolic Letter *Summorum Pontificum*," July 7, 2007.

of the ordinary form, by heading off the abuses that are becoming ever more intolerable and ever less condemned by the pastors responsible, but also helps to permeate the whole life of the Church with the "spirit of the liturgy," to use a phrase of Guardini much valued by Benedict XVI. What is the "spirit of the liturgy" if not a triple theological act of faith, hope, and charity on the part of the believer who, amidst the synchronic and diachronic communion of the Mystical Body, adores, praises, implores, and impetrates God, associating himself with the priestly action of Christ who eternally renews His Sacrifice through the Holy Mass?

Among the innumerable merits that grace the *Vetus Ordo*, one of the most essential is its theocentrism. If the Church's liturgy, the *culmen et fons* of all her life (according to the famous and felicitous expression of the conciliar document *Sacrosanctum Concilium*[6]), survives its anthropocentric crisis and restores primacy to Christ, then a great breath of the Holy Spirit will renew the Church, or to use Romano Guardini's expression, there will be a spiritual awakening of souls, which is precisely what the Church needs. Is this not the supreme purpose of pastoral action?

Benedict XVI has reminded us that evangelization and pastoral work are a mystagogical action. Pope Francis makes a similar claim in the Apostolic Exhortation *Evangelii Gaudium*.[7] Evangelization is an action the Church performs entirely oriented to God and awaiting the touch of His grace. This takes place symbolically in the *Vetus Ordo* with the disposition of the priest and the faithful toward the altar and the crucifix *ad*

---

6 "summit and source": *Sacrosanctum Concilium*, n. 10; cf. *Lumen Gentium*, n. 11.

7 Francis, *Evangelii Gaudium*, n. 166.

orientem. The Pope Emeritus has also told us that the liturgy rightly celebrated can block the spread of spiritual illnesses inside the Church, such as its sociological drift, betrayals of the *depositum fidei*, a worldly spirit, the reduction of faith to emotional experience, and adulterous unions with the cultural fashions we are passing through. The *Vetus Ordo* and its venerability, sacrality, and harmonious synthesis between *lex orandi* and *lex credendi* is an antidote and medicine for conserving the purity of the faith and encouraging the spirit of piety, in short, for contributing to the salvation of souls and their sanctification. In the life of the Church, anything else is superfluous.

Dear friends, I draw to a close. Love for the ancient Mass has drawn us very near to the theological and liturgical sensibility of Benedict XVI and has given us a spontaneous sympathy for his teaching. We must make sure this rich magisterial patrimony, both profound and timely, is not forgotten amidst the present crisis that grips the world and spares not the Catholic Church. For the lay faithful who have gratefully received the Motu Proprio *Summorum Pontificum*, the task is anything but easy. But it is an inspiring and necessary task to receive this heritage left to us by Pope Benedict, to guard it, defend it, spread it, and transmit it to the generations of young people who have the right not to be deprived of its intellectual treasures.

−7−
The Tridentine Mass
A CATECHISM FOR OUR TIMES[†]

Dear Friends,

I EXTEND MY WARM THANKS TO THE organizers of this event for their gracious invitation and for the efforts they have so generously expended to make this meeting possible. I also offer my cordial greetings to each one of you who honors this worthy initiative with your presence. I am happy to find myself in Veneto, a land of ancient and deep-rooted religious tradition. In particular, it is a pleasure to come to Vicenza, this noble city where art and culture symbolically come together in the Palladian architectural style, and where the history and life of the people are placed under the protection of the Virgin of Monte Berico. May St Pius X, the holy pope born in Riese, the pope of the catechism and the liturgy, assist and protect us.

In our conversation today, I would like to develop an argument that I consider relevant for our appreciation of the Tridentine Mass, and that shows why its diffusion among the People of God is an urgent task. The argument is that the Tridentine Mass is a sort of catechism that supports the New Evangelization and contributes to the religious instruction of the faithful. You will kindly forgive the form of this talk, which is more like a conversation than a true and proper lecture.

† A LECTURE GIVEN IN VICENZA, FEBRUARY 2018.

THE MISERABLE FAILURE OF CHRISTIAN INITIATION

I would like to begin with a series of statistics relating to the sociology of religion and to theology.

Those Italians who identify as believers, still the overwhelming majority of the population, are ignorant of their religion. In 2014, the results of a sociological study entitled *Rapporto sull'analfabetismo religioso in Italia* [*Report on Religious Illiteracy in Italy*] were published. The study finds that 50% of the population cannot distinguish between Jesus and Moses and that 60% know almost none of the commandments besides the seventh, "Do not steal." They do not even know the first, which is a profession of faith. On more involved questions such as the identification of the three theological virtues, 80% are completely clueless. I can only imagine what the reaction would be to a question such as "what are the six sins against the Holy Spirit?," which would probably require first explaining who the Holy Spirit is! From these and other indicators, such as the increase in the number of people identifying as "atheist," it seems that things in Italy are not much better than they are in other traditionally Catholic countries like Spain or Belgium. To put it in a word, ever since the abandonment of the Catechism of St Pius X and the Tridentine Mass, the Christian initiation of children and adolescents has been a miserable failure.

Some years ago, a book appeared that was very popular with the "pastoralists," a rather curious class in the contemporary ecclesiastical scene. It was called *La Prima Generazione Incredula* [*The First Unbelieving Generation*], and dealt with Italian youth and "teenagers." In actual fact, rather than unbelieving, it would be more accurate to say that they are merely ignorant. They believe vaguely in God, but they are so entirely unnourished by the catechism that they do not know the most fundamental articles of the Catholic faith, despite the fact that many of them have taken between five and seven years of parochial catechesis and religious instruction at school.

Moreover, this crisis of religious instruction is the source of all sorts of dubious beliefs and deplorable moral behaviors. According to the data provided annually by the Italian National Institute of Statistics and the observations of respected sociologists such as Franco Garelli, the once-strong Catholicism of the Italian people is being eroded away. The number of persons who regularly frequent a place of worship is decreasing, with steep losses in the category of 40 to 55 years old. Evidently they do not know that this is a grave sin against the third commandment. Also on the increase is the number of people who approve the legalization of abortion. They do not know that it is a homicide prohibited by the fifth commandment. Now so-called "Catholic adults" casually admit the possibility of civil unions and sodomite relationships. Apparently they are entirely ignorant that there are four sins crying to heaven for vengeance, one of which prohibits relations contrary to nature.

AN UNASSAILABLE FORTRESS OF THE FAITH

Faced with the situation I have briefly described, it will be very useful to recall a sacred principle of the Christian life: according to the classic formula attributed to Prosper of Aquitaine in the 5th century, "legem credendi lex statuat supplicandi,"[1] more commonly expressed in the axiom *lex orandi, lex*

---

1 In full context, Prosper writes: "Let us be mindful also of the sacraments of priestly public prayer, which, handed down by the Apostles, are uniformly celebrated in the whole world and in every Catholic Church, in order that the law of supplication may support the law of believing."

credendi. Significantly, when we revisit several moments in the history of the Church that were crucial for the definition of dogma, we notice that the discrimination between orthodoxy and heterodoxy was made based on the witness of the liturgical sources. For example, in the 4th century when the second-generation Arians, more hostile and stronger than those of the first, denied the divinity of the Holy Spirit, the Cappadocian Fathers put forward a definitive argument: *isotimia*, i.e., the liturgical formula that attributed the same adoration to the three trinitarian hypostases. *E contra*, whenever the *novatores* have wanted to arbitrarily change what we believe, they have taken up the hammer to demolish liturgical structures, as happened so unfortunately in the time of the Protestant Reformation, which has been so naively, inexplicably, and irresponsibly celebrated by eminent prelates on the occasion of the 500th anniversary of its beginning.

As we sit by and watch the gradual, widespread apostasy of members of the clergy, a tragedy that is only amplified by the media, in our suffering we feel the need to be protected by an unassailable fortress of the faith. The Tridentine Mass is this place where the purity of the faith is integrally conserved and mystically transformed into an act of praise and supplication to God. When I speak about faith, I mean both the objective aspect, the *fides quae*, which in the technical language of theology means the things we believe and give our total adhesion to, and also the subjective aspect, the *fides qua*, by which we entrust to God our whole life with all its joys and sorrows, hopes and worries. In recent times, the balance between these two has been tipped in favor of the second, because in the general climate of relativism and indifferentism, we give insufficient attention, not to say outright disapproval, to "doctrine," thinking that it diminishes the thaumaturgic power of the "pastoral," a talisman-word so often abused. In the words of Scripture, "it covereth a multitude of sins."

With all of this in mind, I would like to point out several characteristics of the Mass according to the *Vetus Ordo* that reveal its wonderful capacity to join faith and prayer together in perfect harmony.

EFFECTIVE TRAINING AND EXERCISE IN THE CREED

The central mysteries of the faith are two, as we well know: the unity and Trinity of God, and the Incarnation, Passion, and death of Our Lord Jesus Christ. The Ordinary of the Tridentine Mass communicates these two fundamental truths with its repeated signs of the cross, the double explicit invocation of the Holy Trinity at the Offertory and at the end of the Mass, in the proclamation of the Prologue of the Gospel of John, and, if I may be permitted to take a patristic term for my own use, with its "liturgical economy" of gestures and symbols that represent the mystery of Our Lord's Passion.

Every faithful soul who follows the sacred rites in his missal is familiar with a genuine pearl of our *regula fidei*, found in the words the priest recites *submissa voce* (in a low voice) as he pours a few drops of water into the chalice. They summarize the whole plan of salvation history: creation, sin, Incarnation, redemption, grace, glory, and eternal life:

> Deus, qui humanae substantiae dignitatem mirabiliter condidisti [*creation*] et mirabilius reformasti [*redemption*], da nobis per huius aquae et vini mysterium eius divinitatis esse consortes [*divinization and the life*

of grace], qui humanitatis nostrae fieri dignatus est particeps [*Incarnation*].[2]

For the believer who fights his spiritual combat in order to win the prize of eternal salvation, our Mass provides an effective training and exercise in the fundamentals of the faith: God, One and Three in His mystery of eternal Love, superabundantly revealed in the Incarnation of the Son and His paschal mystery, the masterpiece of salvation history.

This Mass will educate the believer to perceive not only the chief mysteries of the faith but also the entirety of the creed. I will limit myself to a few examples.

The Christian faith is Marian. The Tridentine Mass venerates Mary in the Canon by expressing the Church's Montfortian service to Mary's royal majesty and her admiration for Mary's privileges, and also when the priest bows his head every time her most holy name is pronounced. Moreover, Mariology is at the heart of the Mass because the altar is sanctified by the invisible assistance of the Mother of God. During an exorcism, a demon once said in fury: "She is there!" How can we forget that St John Paul II dedicated a beautiful chapter of his Encyclical *Ecclesia de Eucharistia* to Mary, Mother of the Eucharist?

Another article of the Catholic faith concerns the *novissimi* (the last things), about which a desolating confusion now reigns in the Church, as we can gather merely by listening to a handful of funeral homilies. But the Tridentine Mass does not forget the souls in Purgatory and it is often offered for them. The

2 "O God, who didst wonderfully establish the dignity of human nature, and still more wonderfully didst restore it: grant us, through the mystery of this water and wine, that we may be made sharers of His divinity, who deigned to become a partaker in our humanity."

Tridentine Mass does not censure any mention of hell, but asks God the Father, through the merits of His Son sacrificed on the altar, to free us from eternal damnation and count us among the flock of the elect. It also frequently mentions paradise and the angels and saints who inhabit it, to whose intercession the Church militant entrusts herself.

A correct ecclesiology that respects the ontological distinction between the baptismal and ordained priesthood is represented in every Tridentine Mass, where the faithful learn to understand the dignity of the sacred minister and thereby to understand the fundamental note of the Church that is her association with Christ, High Priest and Head of the Mystical Body. Thus he is saved from the sociological conception to which the Spouse of Christ is reduced by journalism, sadly the only source from which the ordinary Catholic receives news about the Church.

PENETRATED BY THE UNCTION OF THE HOLY SPIRIT

Now I would like to focus on another cluster of reflections showing that the Tridentine Mass is an effective and comprehensive catechism.

The articles of the faith are professed in the context of a liturgical act that deserves to be called traditional in the noblest sense of the term — a thing slowly forged that, beginning in the dawn of apostolic liturgy, has reached the full splendor of its perfection. The use of the Latin language, a language that by its very nature recalls the past, helps the believer to immerse himself in the furrow of Tradition and to feel an enthusiastic diachronic communion with the generations of faithful Christians who have professed, borne witness to, and communicated the same faith. The *communio sanctorum* is powerfully tangible in the Tridentine Mass! The saints, the most eminent members of the Mystical Body, are united around the sanctifying act *par excellence* that is the Sacrifice of Calvary ritualized upon the altar, sharing with us in the holy realities of the faith. The faith we profess today in our liturgy is knit together with that of the martyrs, confessors, virgins, and the innumerable crowds of the saints, projecting itself toward the beatific vision of the coming eternity of heaven. In the traditional Mass, the faith is "armored" by holy gestures and words that gush up from a mind entirely penetrated by the unction of the Holy Spirit — the mind of the Fathers and Doctors of the Church — and rendered invulnerable to the assaults of the Enemy who, in his attempt to rip the faith from the believer's heart, has resorted to every form of cunning, including the desacralizing application of the liturgical reform that is now apparent to everyone today. The liturgical abuses by which pastors, sometimes through pride, sometimes through ignorance, and sometimes through both, assault the sanctity and sacrality of the Mass have perverted its nature and loaded it with purposes alien to the Catholic faith. The Tridentine Mass, which brings with it an exact observance of the rubrics, protects this treasure of the faith from pillage and squandering.

Because the *Vetus Ordo Missae* transmits the faith in a liturgical context that bears with it an integral vision of man and God and man before God, it is a fitting context for the task of catechesis. Requiring the faithful to remain kneeling for a considerable part of the sacred action and requiring the priest to genuflect before entering into contact with the consecrated host and chalice, the Tridentine Mass teaches that the most appropriate attitude of man toward the Mystery of God is adoration, which as its etymology suggests is an act of loving submission, reverent obedience, and affectionate acceptance of

His majesty. Man recognizes and feels himself to be a creature whose beginning and end are found in and oriented toward the Creator. If this vision is rejected, there can only be an illusive and arrogant anthropocentrism, one that has produced so many wounds and sorrows in the last two centuries, one that banishes hope from men's hearts, as Pope Benedict XVI has taught in his Encyclical *Spe Salvi*. Here permit me to cite a passage from the book of the great Cardinal Robert Sarah, significantly entitled *God or Nothing*. Speaking of the French Spiritan fathers from whom he learned the faith, the African cardinal recalls:

> How many times I was profoundly gripped by the silence that reigned in the church during the Fathers' prayers! At first, settled in the back of the building, I watched these men and wondered what they were doing, kneeling or sitting in the half-light, not saying anything. . . . But they seemed to be listening and conversing with someone in the semi-darkness of the church, lit by candles. I was truly fascinated by their practice of prayer and the peaceful atmosphere it engendered. I think that it is fair to say that there is a true heroism, greatness, and nobility in this life of regular prayer. Man is great only when he is on his knees before God.[3]

This attitude of humble adoration is what instills in believers the fear of God, one of the gifts of the Holy Spirit so little asked for in our days. In proportion to our forgetfulness of this gift,

3 Robert Cardinal Sarah, *God or Nothing: A Conversation on Faith with Nicolas Diat*, trans. Michael J. Miller (San Francisco: Ignatius Press, 2015), 36.

we experience an obscuring of our moral conscience that justifies, both juridically and morally, every kind of transgression against the commandments of God. Man learns on his knees to obey God and His precepts. Morals are just as much a part of catechesis as the creed.

CATECHESIS THROUGH SILENCE AND IMAGES

If the Mass is a catechetical instruction that welds together the *lex orandi, lex credendi,* and *lex vivendi,* it is also important to consider the proper method by which its contents may be well understood and received. The Tridentine Mass has its own catechetical method: silence and images.

Most important of all is the silence that so majestically and sublimely accompanies the sacred rites, especially in the most solemn and sacred moment of the Canon and consecration. Silence aids recollection and encourages personal prayer, thereby assisting the believer to assimilate the *mysteria fidei.* How can we fail to mention the warning posed to us by the Cardinal Prefect of the Congregation for Divine Worship in his book-interview, *The Power of Silence: Against the Dictatorship of Noise*? Without silence, we cannot listen to God; without silence there is no divine intimacy. The words of God are the source of every catechism. Silence is the only way teaching can be received by an intelligence that seeks truth and cherished by a heart that loves it. Cardinal Sarah writes:

> We need to cultivate silence and to surround it with an interior dike. In my prayer and in my interior life, I have always felt the need for a deeper, more complete silence. I am talking about a kind of discretion that amounts to not even thinking about myself but,

rather, turning my attention, my being, and my soul toward God. Sacred silence permits man joyfully to hand himself over to the service of God and is the only truly human, and Christian, reaction when faced with God's irruption into our lives. We must rediscover the profound link between sacred silence and mystery, because without mystery we are reduced to the banality of earthly things. Silence is an acoustic veil that protects the mystery. In the Church's liturgies, silence cannot be a pause between two rituals. Silence is the fabric from which all our liturgies must be cut. Nothing in them should interrupt the silent atmosphere that is its natural setting.[4]

The cardinal has called for a form of spiritual resistance in the face of the daily invasion of words and noises that paralyze thought and render it flat, banal, and uncritical. Unfortunately, the liturgical reform was carried out under the banner of a prolix and vacuous verbalism. It talks about everything, about sociology and political fashions, but very often this loquacious liturgy stifles the small, gentle voice of God knocking softly on the doors of the soul, and buries the *lex orandi/lex credendi* under a cascade of directions, commentary, and free interventions of the faithful.

The catechetical method of the Tridentine Mass is supported by its use of sacred images, both fixed and moving images. Let me explain: the crucifix, the statues of the Madonna and saints, the colors and the walls, everything that catches the eye helps the

4   Robert Cardinal Sarah with Nicolas Diat, *The Power of Silence: Against the Dictatorship of Noise,* trans. Michael J. Miller (San Francisco: Ignatius Press, 2017), 76.

faithful learn the alphabet of the faith, because word and image together speak an effective language. There are also moving images: the "sacred dance" that the priest and ministers perform when they observe the sober, harmonious ritual gestures of the rite. These leave an impression on the hearts of those who assist at Holy Mass. The music and sacred chant are another potent means by which the truths of the faith may be deliciously tasted and digested by the internal faculties of the soul. Indeed, the liturgy of the Roman rite in the *usus antiquior* is an excellent model of catechesis, in both content and form.

Dear friends, I have come to my conclusion. In this reflection I have denounced the plague of religious ignorance. The remedy consists in the diffusion of the *Vetus Ordo Missae*. Following the Second Vatican Council, a courageous and unfortunately ignored bishop asserted that the abolition of the Mass of the Ages and the reckless iconoclasm that came with it had led to the collapse of catechesis, asceticism, and the moral life. We should be very grateful to the Pope Emeritus for his prophetic foresight in promoting the recovery of the Mass of the old rite. He intuited that, just as its suppression had had dramatic repercussions for the whole edifice of the faith, so its restoration, graciously guaranteed by the Motu Proprio *Summorum Pontificum* and promoted by groups of faithful and priests ever more numerous and motivated, would bring with it copious and delicious fruits that would aid in the reconstruction of the ecclesial fabric and promote an authentic renewal of the spiritual life, which must always be our primary concern. If the crisis of the Church is above all a liturgical crisis, as then Cardinal Ratzinger warned and as other learned and holy pastors have recently reminded us, then it is precisely from the reform of the liturgical reform that rebirth will come and the authentic good of the Church will be promoted: the glory of God and the sanctification of souls, "ad laudem et gloriam nominis sui, ad utilitatem quoque nostram totiusque ecclesiae suae sanctae."[5]

5 "to the praise and glory of His Name, to our own benefit, and to that of all His Holy Church."

−8−

"Liturgical Beauty and Joyful Evangelization" (EG 24)

THE EXPERIENCE OF THE TRIDENTINE MASS†

Honored ladies, distinguished gentlemen,

I
T IS A GREAT JOY FOR ME TO SPEAK this evening in the artistic setting of the church of Saints Simon and Jude, in a city so rich in history, culture, and faith—Mantua, a city that boasts so many illustrious citizens: Virgil, "quel savio gentil, che tutto seppe";[1] Sordello, the troubadour who inspired the Supreme Poet's invective against Italy, "di dolore ostello, nave senza nocchiere in gran tempesta,"[2] a sentiment which is true today more than ever; Vittorino da Feltre, Christian pedagogue; the Gonzaga princes, who gathered famous artists in their court, among them the composer Claudio Monteverdi. The four-hundred-fiftieth anniversary of this eminent musician's birth is related to another event. In 2017, we celebrate the tenth anniversary of the publication of the Motu Proprio *Summorum Pontificum* by which Pope Benedict XVI restored dignity to the venerable Tridentine

---

1   "That gentle sage, who knew all things" (*Inferno*, Canto VII).
2   "Inn of sorrows, ship without a helmsman in harsh seas" (*Purgatorio*, Canto VI), trans. Mandelbaum.

† A LECTURE GIVEN IN MANTUA, SEPTEMBER 30, 2017.

liturgy, calling it the "extraordinary form" of the Roman rite. Reflecting on the characteristics of this liturgical form, a passage from the Apostolic Exhortation *Evangelii Gaudium* comes to mind as a springboard for this conversation:

> Evangelization with joy becomes beauty in the liturgy, as part of our daily concern to spread goodness. The Church evangelizes and is herself evangelized through the beauty of the liturgy, which is both a celebration of the task of evangelization and the source of her renewed self-giving.[3]

I would like to develop my thoughts in two points: the Tridentine liturgy is beautiful, and its beauty powerfully evangelizes.

THE TRIDENTINE LITURGY IS BEAUTIFUL

We might say that there have been two complementary conceptions of beauty in the history of Western civilization. The first considers beauty as the *pulchrum*, a proportion and harmony of parts, the perfection of form, integrity, and elegance. It is an Apollonian conception found especially in the art of Greece. It appeals to reason and insists on the objectivity of the beautiful. The other conception, expounded especially by Kant, interprets beauty as a *species*, a sort of luminosity that breaks in upon an object, expands its substance, orienting it outside of itself and putting it in relation with the subject. The whole is in the fragment, as Hans Urs von Balthasar would have said, that great Swiss theologian who, in his monumental work *The Glory of the Lord,* developed a convincing re-reading of

3   Pope Francis, *Evangelii Gaudium*, n. 24.

theology in an aesthetic key. It is not by chance that there was a great harmony of thought and feeling between Hans Urs von Balthasar, theologian of beauty, and Joseph Ratzinger, pope of the liturgy and vindicator of the rights of the Latin Mass. They share a Dionysian conception of beauty that appeals to the senses and focuses on the subject. Both these aesthetic conceptions are in agreement that beauty is always very attractive. For this very reason, in Thomistic philosophy it is associated with the other transcendentals of being — unity, truth, and goodness — as part of the moral and spiritual fruition of the subject who experiences it. Now if we apply these categories to the Tridentine liturgy, we will easily grasp why it is beautiful.

The Tridentine liturgy is harmonious. Like a perfect diptych, its first panel opens with the "Mass of the Catechumens," and its second with the "Mass of the Faithful." The second part is the more important since during it the Sacrifice is offered, and so it also lasts longer. The first part has its own inner coherence: it humbly leads us into the presence of God through the prayers at the foot of the altar, with their sublime penitential orientation. Out of this humility, which is the proper basis of the relationship between creature and Creator, sinner and Redeemer, springs the supplication of the Kyrie and the prayer of the Collect. At this point, we are ready to be instructed by the Wisdom of God that is revealed in salvation history and unfolds the truth that leads us to heaven, for only the humble will "hear" and be glad, as the Psalm says (Ps 33:3). We find a copious sprinkling of Scripture passages and Psalm verses — a *prayed* Bible! — that make up the text of the Introit, Gradual, Tract, Alleluia, and then the pericopes of the Epistle and the Holy Gospel. In every place we find the proportion that is the intrinsic property of beauty: texts that, except on a few special occasions, are neither too long nor too many, as is the case with the biennial or triennial cycle of the *Novus Ordo*. Though it had the laudable intention of offering a semi-continuous reading of the entirety of Sacred Scripture, this cycle ends up "wasting" a great number of texts that the average layman cannot remember and, sometimes, cannot even hear, not only because of the length and difficulty of certain passages, but also because they are read by lectors insufficiently prepared for their task, chosen in obedience to the equality called for by an erroneous understanding of *actuosa participatio*. Length and bad diction are signs of vulgarity, not beauty.

The Offertory begins. The sacred silence and the kneeling position of the faithful give the moment its peculiar solemnity. The prayers of the priest have an especially harmonious structure: the offering of the host and chalice, the personal preparations, the prayer to the Most Holy Trinity. As these ancient and venerable prayers are being offered, they are accompanied by the precise, delicate gestures typical of the Tridentine liturgy, which give the rite its unmistakable *pulchritudo*. These gestures are just one example of the ordered variety that makes the *Vetus Ordo* liturgy so truly beautiful. There are also the bows toward the Cross, the kissing of the cruets by the ministers and of the altar by the priest, and even the affectionate glances toward the sacred vessels and their contents. Christ, Our Lord, is loved because He is beautiful and is beautiful because He is loved. I could go on showing how the extraordinary form of the Roman rite is beautiful because it unfolds without excess or imperfection, with calm and proportion like a melodious chant. But we should move on to other considerations.

Let us try to apply the other conception of beauty to the Tridentine liturgy. The senses of one who assists at it are touched by the Sacred, the *mysterium tremendum et fascinans*, to use the famous definition of Rudolf Otto. They are pervaded by a thrill of spiritual joy, to invoke the great bard of the divine beauty, Augustine of Hippo. The Sacred, that is, the perception of God that follows His manifestation, excites both reverence and adoration, because He is *tremendum*; and love and attraction, because He is *fascinans*. Can anyone deny that reverence and adoration are especially present in the Tridentine liturgy, while unfortunately they are not well preserved in the *Novus Ordo*? Who would not agree with the claim that the priest (mark you, the priest, the *sacrum dans* and not the president of the assembly), the ministers, and the faithful are all intimately drawn (while each remains in his proper place) toward the center of all and everything: the Crucified One enthroned on the altar, where the Sacrifice of the Cross is presented to everyone's gaze, so that everyone may love it? This manifestation of the Sacred, transcendence and immanence, heaven and earth, divine and human, is not merely the religious archetype identified by Otto, but the Incarnation of the divine Word that wills to use the Sacred to reveal His beauty in a human form: the divine Person of Our Lord Jesus Christ, who has united human nature to His divine nature, and thus rendered His divinity accessible to human senses. This logic of the Incarnation extends to the sacred liturgy because, as the Fathers of the Church taught and as the *Catechism of the Catholic Church* has recalled in a timely manner, "quod redemptoris nostri conspicuum fuit, in sacramenta transivit."[4] Beauty strikes the senses, and the Tridentine liturgy strongly affirms the aesthetic dimension.

---

4   "what was visible in our Savior has passed over into His mysteries": CCC, n. 1115, citing Pope St Leo I, *Sermon* 74, 2.

In the Latin Mass, our view is directed to a triple focal point: the crucifix, the altar and what takes place there, and the tabernacle. Our attention is seized by the fairest among the children of men: "they will look upon the one whom they have pierced" (Jn 19:37). Our eyes linger, feasting on the beauty of the colors of the walls, their costly ornament. We follow the ministers' sacred dance, sober and constrained to careful, rhythmic movements, and from time to time our eyes wander to the decoration of the Temple, which recounts, in various styles, the story of the salvation recalled in each Holy Mass. We hear words uttered in a raised voice, in a language different from our ordinary language, because it is reserved for dialogue with God, like a code that heightens understanding and connection between those who adopt it, a sort of familial register sons use to address their Father. It is a beautiful language, as only Latin can be, with its figures of sound and word, with a compact but still mobile construction that comes from its unmistakable literary style. Further, we hear the great silence that shrouds the priestly prayers, above all the *Canon Missae*, because the Mystery of God who pours out His blood for me, a sinner, because He loves me and saves me, can only be uttered *submissa voce*. He loves silence as He loves all great and sublime things — the silence that invites everyone to recollection and earnest prayer. The sense of hearing opens for the soul the enchantments of sacred music, the sound of the organ, the Gregorian chant, and in this way the soul is mystically lifted on high. We smell the fragrant perfume of the incense that rises to heaven just like our prayer, and the odor of the candles, symbols of the hearts that pine with longing for heaven. All this proclaims a hope that the world does not know — and that the Church of the last few years, not comprehending the grandeur of the *Vetus Ordo*, seems herself to have forgotten. Immersed in secular matters, and entranced by transient fashions, she has become like chaff scattered in the wind.

The sense of touch is also involved: kneeling at various points in the Holy Mass permits the faithful to touch the earth, and from this position to render adoration, thanksgiving, supplication, and impetration. The sense of touch is denied contact with the Eucharistic species because the consecrated Host is received directly on the tongue, an eloquent gesture that expresses all the sanctity of the Sacrament received with faith. Only the priest is permitted to touch the Body and Blood of Christ, and only with extreme delicacy, as if caressing it. In fact, on the day of his priestly ordination, his hands were anointed with the chrism, a biblical-liturgical sign of the Holy Spirit, the divine Person who through the epiclesis performs that miracle of miracles, the consecration. "Taste and see that the Lord is good!" (Psalm 33:9), the Psalmist exclaims. The *Vetus Ordo* liturgy frequently repeats this verse to dispose the faithful to partake of the Body and Blood of Christ with a hunger at once spiritual and material, provided they are suitably disposed to do so.

To sum up, dear friends, we must find, perceive, and enjoy the beauty of the One who has been pierced. This is a "synesthetic" experience that affirms sensual richness — for the sacraments are *propter homines* ("for us men"), as Thomas Aquinas would say — so that the manifestation of the All in the fragment, of God in the space and time of the unbloody renewal of the sacrifice *hic et nunc*, may irradiate the Divine Mystery that is in itself the revelation of beauty. Confronted with this liturgy that is so potently theocentric and therefore respectful of all anthropological structures, we cannot help but remark, with a note of sadness, that the *Novus Ordo* is more impoverished, more rational, more prolix, even to the point that it becomes irritatingly and insufferably wordy in the hands of certain showman priests and ministers. A liturgy celebrated in this way is relentlessly narcissistic and vulgar.

Permit me to conclude this point about the beauty of the old liturgy with a Marian reflection. Our Lady, *Tota Pulchra*, the All-Beautiful, is the creature in whom all beauty, insofar as it is *pulchritudo* and *speciositas*, is concentrated. The Tridentine liturgy cannot help but invoke her in the heart of the Mass: in the prayer that offers the sacrifice to the Most Holy Trinity, and in the *Communicantes* of the Canon. An irrepressible longing for heaven rises from the thought of the Holy Virgin, who descends more beautiful than the dawn (Cant 6:9) to soften the pains of this life, where we can always count on her powerful patronage.

THE BEAUTY OF THE TRIDENTINE LITURGY AND EVANGELIZATION

Recall the opening citation from *Evangelii Gaudium*, which pointed out the relationship between the *via pulchritudinis* of the liturgy and the twofold evangelical movement of the Church. The Church first allows herself to be evangelized so that she can then evangelize the world. Let us explicate this point.

More than ever, the Church today needs to be oriented to Christ, her Head, her Spouse, her Founder. Christ is her Gospel, the good news that brings joy to her youth and fills her with authentic joy and hope. Unfortunately in the past few years, with a rapidity that should raise serious questions and concern, the Church has become engrossed with issues of a sociological nature, all affecting more or less the Church's moral teaching. Many dubious proposals have been made by pastors, even those who bear serious ecclesial responsibilities, that are frankly incompatible with the Gospel. The Church feels the need to be re-evangelized and led back to Christ. Pope Benedict XVI made extraordinary efforts in this direction, and his trilogy on Jesus of Nazareth is an expression of a Christocentrism founded on Scripture and the sound doctrine of Tradition. He always wanted to promote a reform of the liturgy, and this program found a great expression in *Summorum Pontificum*.

The Tridentine Mass is truly evangelical because it is Christocentric. Just think of its conclusion: the proclamation of the prologue of the Gospel of John. It is like a hinge joining the liturgy to the daily life to which we are about to return. It proclaims the heart of the Gospel, the mystery of the Incarnation, with the beauty we have been speaking of: the hieratic movement of the priest toward the *cornu evangelii* ("the Gospel side"), the reading, the genuflection at the words "et Verbum caro factum est," and during the Sung Mass, the musical piece performed by the *schola cantorum*. The Church is evangelized during the celebration of the Tridentine Mass because, as the fourth-century Father of the Church and author of very valuable liturgical-mystagogical catecheses, Cyril of Jerusalem, said, the teachings of Sacred Scripture must be gathered into a summary, the *regula fidei* ("the rule of faith"), the Creed of the catechism — and the Tridentine Mass is this catechism in action, tying us intimately to the Gospel of Christ. "What are the two principal mysteries of the faith?" asked the unsurpassable Catechism of St Pius X. The Mass itself tells us. We profess our faith in God's unity and Trinity when we turn to the three divine Persons at the beginning of the Mass in the ninefold Kyrie, three times invoking the Father, three times Christ, and three times the Spirit. We adore their majesty when we sing the Gloria. We implore them to accept our offering at the Offertory.

We express our desire for them to accept the sacrifice in the prayer just before the final blessing. As for the mystery of Our Lord's Incarnation, Passion, and death: how many signs of the cross does the priest trace out, especially during the Canon? The whole ancient liturgy and all of its texts are steeped in the theology of the Fathers of the Church, rather than the ideas of the experts and specialists of the twentieth century, and its rites are a compendium of the Holy Gospel, the Church's real treasure that has been translated into doctrine and summarized in the catechism.

We could continue to multiply examples of how the Tridentine Mass is a catechism for everyone, including believing evangelizers and non-believers in need of evangelization. The plan of salvation history — creation, sin, Incarnation, redemption, grace, glory, and eternal life — is taken up and synthesized in the great prayers of the Church. For instance, think of the words that the priest says as he pours the water into the chalice:

> Deus, qui humanae substantiae dignitatem mirabiliter condidisti [*creation*] et mirabilius reformasti [*redemption*], da nobis per huius aquae et vini mysterium eius divinitatis esse consortes [*divinization and the life of grace*], qui humanitatis nostrae fieri dignatus est particeps [*Incarnation*].⁵

Now take the *Confiteor*. The ritual gestures surrounding it recall the whole drama of sin with great clarity and poignancy,

5 "O God, who didst wonderfully establish the dignity of human nature, and still more wonderfully didst restore it: grant us, through the mystery of this water and wine, that we may be made sharers of His divinity, who deigned to become a partaker in our humanity."

as we kneel, beat our chests, recite the prayer, and await the priest's absolution so sadly abolished in the *Novus Ordo*: "Indulgentiam, absolutionem, et remissionem peccatorum vestroum tribuat vobis omnipotens et misericors Dominus."[6] In the Roman Canon, the priest asks the Father for the grace to pass through the final judgment, the judgment that should be our only concern, albeit a serene one, because Mary is praying for us: "ab aeterna damnatione nos eripi et in electorum tuorum iubeas grege numerari."[7]

Once she has been evangelized, the Church is ready to evangelize. The Tridentine Mass furnishes the grace that makes her disciples into zealous apostles, and her faithful into courageous missionaries. Is this not the Mass that inspired generation upon generation of our forefathers to spread the Gospel to faraway lands, often in the midst of grave dangers? When we read the chronicles of the missionary expeditions of the Jesuits and Franciscans in Asia and Latin America in the seventeenth and eighteenth centuries, we realize, not without admiration and emotion, that their overriding concern was to offer the Sacrifice of the Mass, using a liturgical form that awaits everything from God as a gift, including the grace of the effectiveness of the work of evangelization.

The *usus antiquior* is an effective evangelizer for another reason: it speaks to the heart of those who have lost the faith or never had it. For example, today in our Western society that denies its Christian roots, some people, thirsting for recollection and interior peace, turn to Oriental philosophies that, despite

6 "May the almighty and merciful Lord grant you pardon, absolution, and remission of your sins."
7 "Snatch us from eternal damnation and command that we be numbered among the flock of Thine elect."

whatever good is in them, leave the soul in its existential lone-liness. They have no God to love them, to feel loved by, to love in return. The silence and sacrality of the Tridentine Mass is a discovery that often becomes the first step toward the faith. Others, especially the young, find our "pastoral initiatives" banal, if not outright heterodox. They are looking for solid spiritual food. The Tridentine Mass offers them this substantial nour-ishment. Its theology coincides completely with the *fides quae* ("what is believed"); here the *lex orandi* is the *lex credendi.* The simple, who are the beloved of God, intuitively recognize that something very great is taking place in the Tridentine Mass, where the priests speaks with God and all are on their knees before Him. In this way, they, too, are taught and evangelized by the sacred mysteries. Every kind of person feels the fascina-tion of the splendor of this Mass, which is always solemn and majestic even when offered in a small place or with modest means, because it is truly beautiful — beautiful with a beauty mediated through vestments, words, gestures, but founded in God, the supremely beautiful. To be at this Mass is to set out on a Platonic *itinerarium pulchritudinis in Deum,*[8] which begins from material signs and ascends in steps up to Reality itself. It gazes upon creation in order to rise to the creator. The experience was described by Augustine, and I will close our conversation with his words:

> Question the beauty of the earth, question the beauty
> of the sea, question the beauty of the air, amply
> spread around everywhere, question the beauty of the
> sky, question the serried ranks of the stars, question

8 A journey to God along the path of beauty.

the sun making the day glorious with its bright beams, question the moon tempering the darkness of the night with its shining rays, question the animals that move in the waters, that amble about on dry land, that fly in the air; their souls hidden, their bodies evident; the visible bodies needing to be controlled, the invisible souls controlling them; question all these things. They all answer you, "Here we are, look: we are beautiful." Their beauty is their confession. Who made these beautiful changeable things, if not unchanging Beauty?[9]

9   Augustine, *Sermon* 241. Translation slightly modified from the Vatican website: http://www.vatican.va/spirit/documents/spirit _20000721_agostino_en.html.

ABOUT THE AUTHOR

FR. ROBERTO SPATARO, S.D.B., is a professor of ancient Greek Christian literature on the faculty of Christian and Classical Literature at the Pontifical Salesian University, and secretary of the *Pontificia Academia Latinitatis.* He has licentiate and doctoral degrees in dogmatic theology from the same university and has published in the fields of Patristics (especially Origen), Mariology, and Latin history, linguistics, pedagogy, and liturgy.